A Beginner's Guide to Forensic Science

quantum scientific publishing

A Beginner's Guide to Forensic Science

Susan M. Carlson

Carly A. Pietrzyk, PhD

quantum scientific publishing

A Beginner's Guide to Forensic Science

ISBN-13: 978-1494294960
ISBN-10: 1494294966

Published by quantum scientific publishing

Pittsburgh, PA | Copyright © 2013

Cover design by Scott Sheariss

QUANTUM
SCIENTIFIC
PUBLISHING

Table of Contents

Chapter 1 – Forensic Sciences and Their History

Chapter Objective

- Describe forensic sciences and summarize the history of the field

What are the forensic sciences?

Forensic science is the application of science as it relates to the law. Any science can become a forensic science. Any field of the medical, behavioral and physical sciences may be applied as a forensic science. Forensic sciences use the methods and laws of scientific inquiry to collect and analyze evidence from crimes. The results from these investigations are used to develop and try criminal cases in the courts.

Although any branch of science may be applied as a forensic science, there are two that are most commonly used to investigate crimes. These are physical sciences and medical sciences.

Within the physical sciences, physics and chemistry have the most application to forensics. Physical sciences are important in understanding bullet trajectories, tool marks, blood spatter and understanding the force involved in a crime. Chemistry techniques are used to analyze all sorts of evidence, from illegal drugs to carpet fibers. Chemistry is also used to isolate and identify DNA, which has become an important tool in the forensic sciences.

The medical sciences are essential to understanding what the body has to tell about the cause of death. Physiology, anatomy, toxicology, and many other medical disciplines are key to deciphering the cause of death. Wounds give clues to what harmed or killed the victim. The condition of the body can give clues to the time and manner of death. It can also help the forensic scientist determine if the body was moved after death or not. Toxicology is used to determine whether any poisons or other compounds contributed to the death. X-rays and other imaging techniques can be used to identify injuries, as well as possibly to identify the victim. Dental records and surgical implants often have serial numbers that can be traced back to the hospital and the patient.

Pistol being fired. Courtesy of the Maine State Police

Forensic sciences have developed over thousands of years. One of the first applications of forensics was fingerprinting. The ancient Chinese used fingerprints to identify business documents. How is this related to forensics? Business documents are legal documents, whichmeans that fingerprintswill be key evidence if there is a dispute. The first system for classifying fingerprints was developed by Sir Francis Galton in 1892. This was soon followed by another system that was based on the characteristics of fingerprints (direction, flow, pattern, etc.) and was developed by Sir Edward Henry, who was commission of the Metropolitan Police of London. Sir Henry's system is the standard for fingerprinting systems worldwide. Today forensic scientists have access to databases of information that help them solve crimes. The automated fingerprint identification system (AFIS) was developed in the 1960s. AFIS is used to find matches to fingerprints from crime scenes. AFIS accesses the FBI database of fingerprints to find a match to the one from the crime scene. These computers are able to scan through 500,000 prints in less than a second.

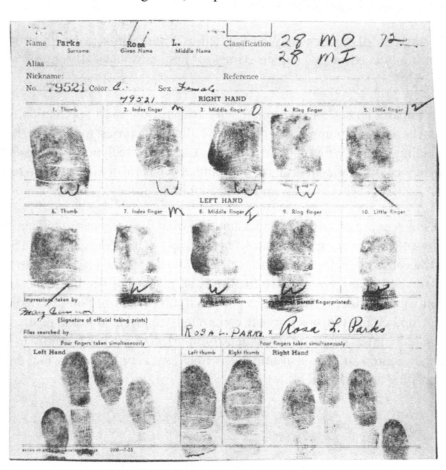

Fingerprint Card of Rosa Parks
Civil Case 1147 Browder, et al v. Gayle, et. al; U.S. District Court for Middle District of Alabama, Northern (Montgomery) Division Record Group 21: Records of the District Court of the United States National Archives and Records Administration-Southeast Region, East Point, GA.

The first ballistics analysis was done in 1835 by Henry Goddard of Scotland Yard. He was able to connect a bullet to the murder weapon. This field was further refined in the 1920s when the comparison microscope was developed by Calvin Goddard. This microscope allows a forensic scientist to figure out which bullets came from which shell casings. Much later, in the 1970s, a technique for detecting gunshot residue with a scanning electron microscope was developed.

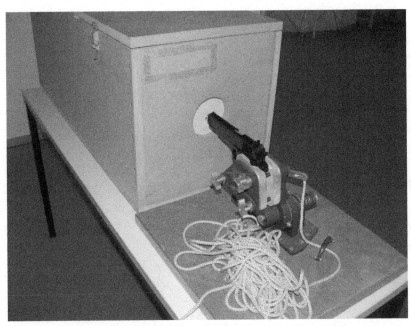

A box used to test ballistics. Image courtesy of Rama.

Scientists continued to develop tests to detect different chemicals. The field of forensic toxicology was born in 1821 when scientists used a chemical technique to find arsenic in the stomach and urine of people who were poisoned. Today, toxicology is used to identify and analyze foreign compounds found in the body. These compounds may be prescription drugs, illegal drugs, poisons, or anything else the victim ingested (drank or ate). Many mystery stories and television shows focus on exotic poisons that are hard to detect because they add interest to the story. In real life, however, poisoning is often accidental. The skull and crossbones symbol on containers of cleaners and other chemicals indicate a poisonous compound. Forensic toxicology is a broad discipline. It includes the study of the thousands of toxic compounds (including poisons) that exist. It also borrows from many other scientific fields, including biochemistry, epidemiology, physiology, analytical chemistry and others. A forensic toxicologist must have a broad understanding of toxic substances, the physical characteristics of those substances, and how the body responds to them.

Again, scientists continued to develop new techniques in the lab that were applied to forensic investigations. For example, the work done by Karl Landsteiner to classify human blood into groups was the starting point for using blood in criminal investigations. Since then, tests have been developed to analyze body fluids, such as saliva and semen. Blood tests have been refined to be more precise.

DNA testing has been a huge addition to forensic sciences and crime scene investigation. Alec Jeffreys and his research team from Leicester University discovered that each person has unique DNA. No one else has the same combination of DNA molecules. After this discovery, Jeffreys' team went on to develop a technique called DNA Fingerprinting, which is also known as DNA typing. This is used to identify individuals from samples that contain DNA.

DNA; Courtesy of Genome Management Information System,
Oak Ridge National Laboratory

Forensic sciences have been developing for thousands of years. As technology has developed, it has been applied to problems of forensics. Computers, imaging technologies, databases, and many other technologies have contributed to better and more precise forensic investigation tools.

Summary

Forensic science is the application of science as it relates to the law. Physical science and medical sciences are the two most commonly applied forensic sciences. The forensic sciences have developed over thousands of years. One of the first applications was in China, where business documents would be marked with fingerprints. As technology improved, the application of technology to forensic investigations has helped the police solve crimes.

· ·

Concept Reinforcement

1. Define forensic sciences.

2. List the two sciences most commonly applied to forensics.

3. Describe how forensics developed.

Chapter 2 – The Crime Laboratory

Chapter Objective

- Explain the importance of the organization and services provided by a crime laboratory

The Crime Laboratory–Organization

The crime laboratory is similar to a research or clinical laboratory in many ways. They use many of the same techniques and pieces of equipment. A top-notch crime lab will use state of the art equipment and techniques, as well as having highly trained researchers who collect, protect and analyze the evidence. Because the work done in the crime lab affects criminal proceedings, crime labs are held to an even higher standard. The work done by crime labs must withstand the scrutiny of a defense attorney. The crime lab must maintain extremely high ethical standards and complete compliance with all protocols for handling and analyzing evidence. Any break in ethics or evidence handling protocols can damage the criminal case, potentially resulting in the case being dismissed because the evidence was compromised.

Crime labs are usually part of the police department. This is not always the case, however. Crime labs may also be in the prosecutor or district attorney's offices, be combined with the office of the coroner or Medical Examiner, affiliated with universities, or even be independent agencies.

Crime labs may be full service crime labs or affiliated with other law enforcement or academic organizations. All crime labs are organized slightly differently, depending upon the needs of the area.

Full service crime laboratories are often divided into the following basic service units:

- Physical Science Unit

- Biology Unit

- Firearms Unit (Ballistics)

- Document Examination Unit

- Photography Unit

> **The First US Crime Lab**
>
> August Volmer established the first forensic laboratory in the US in 1923 for the Los Angeles Police Department. He went on to help establish the FBI Crime Lab in 1932.

Full service crime labs may also have the following units.

- Toxicology Unit

- Latent Fingerprint Unit

- Polygraph Unit

- Voiceprint Analysis Unit

- Evidence Collection Unit

Many other forensic sciences may or may not be included in a crime scene. These include forensic arts, computer forensics, digital forensics, explosives, hazardous materials, and many others. Remember that any discipline can be applied in service of the law.

The FBI Crime Laboratory. Courtesy Federal Bureau of Investigation.

The Crime Laboratory–Services

The services provided by crime laboratories depend upon a number of things, including local law, budget and staffing limitations, and the availability of relevant expertise from other organizations. Many crime labs focus only on analyzing drug evidence.

The following material introduces the based components of a crime lab. A large crime lab may have many other specialized units. These include the Physical Sciences Unit, the Biology Unit, the Firearms Unit, the Document Examination Unit and the Photography Unit.

Physical Sciences Unit

The Physical Sciences Unit analyzes the physical evidence from the crime scene. This does not include biological samples. The Physical Science Unit performs tests on samples, such as drugs, glass, paint, soil, and explosives.

Biology Unit

The Biology Unit analyzes the biological evidence from the crime scene. Biological specimens include DNA, body fluids, hair, fiber, and any other biological specimen. They also identify unknown biological specimens.

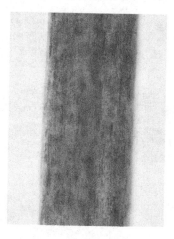

Hair sample for analysis

Firearms Unit (Ballistics)

The Firearms Unit is responsible for identifying the type of gun a bullet was fired from, as well as matching individual bullets to the weapons from which they were fired. This unit examines firearms, bullets, cartridge cases, shotgun shells, and ammunition.

Document Examination Unit

This unit conducts handwriting and typewriting analysis, including computer-generated documents. Any questioned document is sent to this lab for analysis. This unit will also examine any document suspected of holding evidence to a crime, so they specialize in following paper trails. Forgeries, ransom notes, and accounting trails are some examples of examined documents. This unit may also include footwear impressions and tire treads.

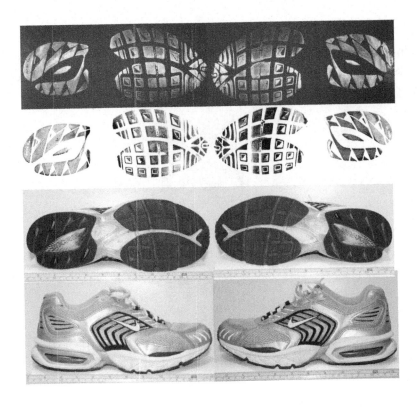

This image shows a series of footwear impressions / shoeprints
recovered from a crime scene. (From Top to bottom)
1- Footwear impressions found at a crime scene.
2- Test footwear impressions made a suspect's footwear.
3- Photo of the outsoles of footwear recovered from a suspect.
4- Photo of the suspect's footwear.
Image courtesy of Zalman992

Photography Unit

This unit performs the essential task of documenting the physical evidence in its original state. The Photography Unit will also examine the physical evidence as it is shown in the photos to help solve the crime. Forensic photographers use a number of tools to perform their work. A good camera is essential, of course. However, a good camera does not ensure good pictures. The forensic photographer is trained to take images of evidence that will be useful in solving the crime. This means the images must show evidence in the context of the crime scene. It also means that the images must be clear and evenly lit so the investigators are able to get as much information as possible from the image. Forensic photographers may also use alternate light sources to find evidence that cannot be seen with the naked human eye. Examples include bodily fluids and gunshot residue. Some fibers even have unique characteristics that show up under different types of light. Photomicrography is used to take highly detailed images of small items, such as bullets or hair, through a microscope. Photography is even important for analyzing impression evidence, such as tire impressions. Images of the impression can be used to compare evidence directly with whatever is suspected of making the impression. High quality images are important both for analysis and for presentation to the court during trial.

Summary

The crime laboratory may be organized in a number of different ways. These include crime labs that are part of a larger law enforcement organization. Crime labs may also be part of an academic institution, such as a university, or be independent organizations. Each crime lab offers different services, depending upon the needs of local law enforcement. A full-service crime lab will often have a physical science unit, a biology unit, a ballistics unit, a questioned documents unit, and a photography unit. Each of these units plays a key role in collecting, protecting and analyzing crime scene evidence.

. . . .

Concept Reinforcement

1. Explain how a crime lab differs from a research or clinical lab.

2. Describe how a full-service crime lab might be organized.

3. Discuss the role of the physical sciences unit in a crime lab.

Chapter 3 – Careers in the Forensic Sciences

Chapter Objective

- Discuss the different careers in forensic sciences

Careers in Forensic Sciences

There are many careers in the forensic sciences. Job titles include criminalist, crime scene investigator, forensic investigator, forensic pathologist, forensic pathology technician, forensic anthropologist, forensic toxicologist, fingerprint examiner, forensic document examiner, and forensic medical transcriber, among many others.

Forensic Investigator

A forensic investigator, also known as a coroner's investigator, goes to the crime scene when someone dies and is responsible for collecting the body for further examination by the coroner. When a forensic investigator gets to the crime scene, she is responsible for preparing the body for transport, trying to identify the body, collecting any personal belongs present, and interviewing friends, family members or others who may have witnessed the crime. A forensic investigator may collect evidence from the body before transport and may have to prepare written reports about his actions and may even have to testify in court. This job requires at least a high school diploma (or equivalent). It also requires some experience in law enforcement or investigative work, as well as a basic understanding of evidence collection, evidence preservation, chain-of-custody, and the related laws. Many people prepare for this position by becoming police officers or getting a degree in forensic sciences.

Forensic Pathology Technician

A pathology technician assists the forensic pathologist in performing autopsies. They may even perform parts of the autopsy. A forensic pathology technician collects samples for toxicology testing, as well as tissues for microscopic examination (histology), blood for blood testing, samples to test for infectious diseases, fingerprints, X-rays, and trace evidence analysis. In some cases, forensic pathology technicians interact with the families of victims and the police. In most cases, a high school diploma is the only requirement for this job, but experience helps a lot, especially experience in a forensic pathology lab. A bachelor's degree in a lab-based discipline helps, as well. To be successful as a forensic pathology technician, you must understand laboratory safety and infection control procedures, know how to use the equipment and tools found in the laboratory, and understand general medical lab procedures.

Fingerprint Examiner

A fingerprint examiner is just what it sounds like. A person in this position is responsible for collecting and analyzing fingerprints. This is a key position in any crime lab. In order to do this job, you must understand how to find, collect and protect fingerprint evidence, as well as how to analyze it and match it to an individual. This position does not typically require a college degree, but it depends on the jurisdiction. It helps to have taken some courses in chemistry, biology, math and other related fields.

FBI Fingerprint examiners at work. Image courtesy of the FBI.

Forensic Medical Transcriber

A forensic medical transcriber is responsible for transcribing oral and written notes on autopsies or other forensic tests. The job also includes other administrative duties like filing, interacting with the public, and record keeping. This is an important position for maintaining the efficiency of the coroner's office and professionalism of the coroner's office. While this position does not require a degree, it does require experience as a secretary or executive assistant and training in medical terminology.

Forensic Document Examiner

A forensic document examiner is responsible for examining document for age, authenticity and authorship. A person in this position must be able to work alone and also be extremely patient and detail-oriented. Skills required include photography, language and lab testing procedures. There is no educational requirement for this job unless you want to be certified by the American Board of Forensic Document Examiners (ABFDE). If you want to obtain this certification, you must have at least a bachelor's degree and a certain amount of work experience.

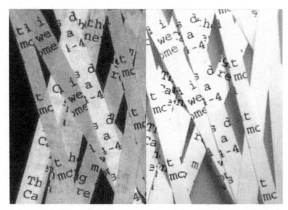

Image of shredded paper produced in UV radiation (left) and white light (right). Notice how shreds have differing luminescent intensities that may help the examiner sort the pieces. Image courtesy of the Federal Bureau of Investigation.

Criminalist

The title Criminalist applies to jobs in many different fields of forensic sciences. Criminalist is a modern term that usually refers to crime scene and crime lab workers. People who are attracted to this field usually enjoy law enforcement and the precision of laboratory work. The basic educational requirement for this job ranges from a high school diploma to a bachelor's degree in forensic science or a laboratory science field (biology, chemistry, etc.). The educational requirement will depend upon the specific field of forensic sciences. It may even be necessary to pursue an advanced degree (masters or doctorate) for specific jobs.

Crime Scene Investigator

These are the people you see portrayed as doing all the work of a criminal investigation on television, from investigating the scene to arresting the suspect. This is not how a crime lab really works. A crime scene investigator, also called a crime scene technician, is responsible for collecting evidence from a crime scene. CSIs are not responsible for questioning or arresting suspects. This involves helping keep the crime scene secure; protecting, preserving and collecting evidence; work the crime scene; recognize evidence; and maintain the chain of custody of the evidence. CSIs collect fingerprint evidence, biological evidence, physical evidence and any other evidence found at the crime scene that might help the police solve the crime. In order to become a CSI, you will need to get a degree in forensic science or become a police officer.

Cambodian students learning how to investigate a crime scene.
Image courtesy of the US Embassy

Forensic Toxicologist

A forensic toxicologist is responsible for testing samples from the dead to determine cause of death. A forensic toxicologist also tests for the presence of drugs, analyzes drugs for their chemical makeup, and tests for any other potentially toxic compound involved in a crime. Toxicology is a combination of chemistry, physiology, biology and pharmacology. It requires you to be familiar with sample collection, lab equipment and the protocols used for analyzing drugs and other compounds. A forensic toxicology position usually requires a bachelor's degree in a lab science at a minimum. Many labs will require an advanced degree.

Forensic Anthropologist

A forensic anthropologist is an expert in many disciplines, including biology, history, anthropology and archaeology. The primary job of a forensic anthropologist is human remains recovery. As with a crime scene investigator, a forensic anthropologist preserves the scene, uses scientific procedures to recover the remains, secures and protects the evidence, and ensures the chain-of-custody of the evidence. In addition, a forensic anthropologist develops biological profiles for the remains, including age, sex, height, race, etc., and assesses cause of death based on the evidence from the skeletal remains. A forensic anthropologist usually has a PhD (doctoral degree) in anthropology or human biology. In order to sit for board exams, you must have at least three years of field experience in addition to the PhD. Forensic anthropologists usually work at universities, an consult with medical examiners offices, police and the courts.

Service members search for POW/MIAs on Wake Island Greg Berg uses a sifter to look for bone and artifacts at a dig site Jan. 12 on Wake Island. Mr. Berg, a forensic anthropologist, was sent to do a site survey after Wake Island officials notified the Joint POW/MIA Accounting Command of bones located on the island. JPAC officials are charged with achieving the fullest possible accounting of all Americans missing as a result of past conflicts. (U.S. Air Force photo/Tech. Sgt. Shane A. Cuomo)

Forensic Pathologist

Forensic pathologists are the people who perform the autopsies of people who died under suspicious circumstances. They are responsible for determining the cause of death for each person they autopsy. They also help the police solve crimes by teasing out the clues the body has to offer about what happened during the crime. A forensic pathologist has to perform autopsies on car crash victims, burn victims, murder victims, and anyone else whose cause of death is unclear. This means that the bodies are often very damaged. Forensic pathologists often testify as expert witnesses during trials and represent the coroner's office in various capacities. A forensic pathologist must have a medical license, along with extensive knowledge about the human body. A forensic pathologist must also know about laboratory testing techniques, evidence rules, court procedures, crime-scene investigation, and criminal law.

A forensic pathologist must have a medical degree, which is followed by a medical internship (1 year) and a pathology residency (4 years). After all this education, you sill need to pass the forensic pathology board exams to be certified in anatomic pathology and forensic pathology if you want to lead the lab. This exam is administered by the American Board of Pathology.

Summary

This section discussed only a few of the jobs that might be involved in forensics. The educational requirements for the jobs range from a high school diploma (or equivalent) to a doctorate with extensive post-doctoral training and board certification. Regardless of your educational goals, if you want to work on crime scenes and help solve crimes, there are jobs that will fit you. All of the positions, regardless of education level, are important to the success of the crime lab.

Concept Reinforcement

1. Name and describe one crime lab job that requires a high school diploma.

2. Explain the educational requirements and experience needed to be a forensic pathologist.

3. Explain why all positions in a crime lab are important to the outcome of the case.

Chapter 4 – Local and State Agencies

Chapter Objective

- Describe the roles of agencies involved in forensic investigations at the local and state levels

Agencies at all levels of government are involved in criminal and forensic investigations. At the local level, these include the police and local crime lab, if one exists. At the state level, the state police and crime labs become involved.

First Responders

The police are usually the first to arrive at a crime scene. Once they have determined that a crime has taken place, they secure the scene and call in the crime scene investigators. The police and the crime scene investigators work together to maintain the security of the crime scene; identify, protect and collect the evidence; ensure the chain of custody for the evidence; and transport it to the crime lab. If a death occurred, the forensic investigator or medical examiner is called to prepare the body for transport, collect evidence from the body, try to identify the body, and interview witnesses.

Police documenting a scene after a violent attack in a home. Courtesy of Andrew Mason, Chester, UK

Resources

The local law enforcement agency may not have the resources necessary to fully process the crime scene. In this case, experts from a nearby jurisdiction or the state police or crime lab are called to collect, protect, transport and/or analyze the evidence.

Big cities will usually have well-developed crime labs that are able to manage any crimes that occur in their jurisdictions. Smaller towns may or may not have anyone with expertise beyond basic crime scene investigation. Law enforcement agencies cooperate extensively in investigating crimes.

State Crime Laboratories

Each state has at least one crime laboratory that serves law enforcement agencies statewide. In Wisconsin, for example, there is a network of three crime labs, which are part of the Wisconsin Department of Justice. These labs are located at key points around the state: Milwaukee, Madison and Wausau. Each lab serves a portion of the state. The Madison lab serves south-central and south-west Wisconsin, as well as the northern part of the state for services that cannot be supplied by the Wausau laboratory. The Milwaukee laboratory serves the southeast part of Wisconsin, which is the most populated. The laboratory in Wausau serves the northern part of Wisconsin.

Wisconsin crime labs are able to perform the following forensic analyses:

Chemistry	Criminalistics	DNA Analysis
Drug Identification	Firearm/Toomark Identification	DNA Databank
Toxicology	Forensic Imaging	DNA Analysis
Trace	Questioned Document	
	Field Response	
	AFIS Specialists	

If the Wisconsin crime lab needs help analyzing evidence, they will go to other state crime labs or the FBI Crime lab for assistance.

Each state has a crime lab, so if you want to learn about your state's system, you should be able to find information on the internet or through your state's Justice Department.

State Patrol

The state patrol is a law enforcement agency that is primarily responsible for highway safety and providing statewide law enforcement services. State patrol agencies provide assistance to local law enforcement if they need help with managing civil disturbances, natural disasters, communications, and chemical testing for drivers suspected of being under the influence of alcohol or other drugs.

Again, using Wisconsin as an example, the State Patrol has four divisions. These are the Communications Bureau, Field Operations Bureau, Transportation Safety Bureau, and State Patrol Academy Office. Each division has a specific role.

The overall role of the Wisconsin State Patrol is to bureau enforce traffic and criminal laws; help motorists who need assistance; inspect trucks, school buses and ambulances; and support local law enforcement agencies if they have to deal with natural disasters or civil disturbances.

Communications Bureau	Field Operations Bureau	Transportation Safety Bureau	Safety Patrol Academy Office
Responsible for the statewide communications network	Enforces traffic and criminal laws	Develops and implements safety programs and safety analysis	Trains State Patrol recruits.
Radio tower sites	Conducts criminal highway interdiction programs	Carries out public outreach on safety issues	Trains federal and local law enforcement officers and state employees.
Voice and data transmission equipment	Assists local law enforcement with traffic safety, civil disturbances and disasters	Administers the statewide chemical testing program	Trains employees from other agencies as appropriate.
Mobile Data Communications Network (MDCN)		Oversees motor carrier safety and weight facilities	
		Inspects and regulates motor carriers, school buses, and ambulances	

Summary

Local and state law enforcement agencies work closely together to investigate and prosecute crimes. Local agencies are usually the first to arrive at and process a crime scene. If the local police and crime lab are not able to analyze all the samples, they ask for assistance from the State Crime Lab. The state police are available to help investigate and prosecute crimes in the state and support local law enforcement as needed.

Concept Reinforcement

1. Describe the role of the first responders to a crime scene.

2. Explain why a local law enforcement agency may not be able to manage a crime scene investigation on its own.

3. Describe the role of the state police and state crime labs in solving crimes.

Chapter 5 – Federal Agencies

Chapter Objective

- Describe the roles of the agencies involved in forensic investigations at the Federal level

The FBI Laboratory

The FBI Laboratory is the primary federal forensics laboratory for the United States and one of the best crime labs in the world. Established in 1932, the FBI Laboratory is now housed in a 500,000 square foot state of the art laboratory in Virginia. The lab sets the standard for security and evidence control. It was designed with specific paths for the acceptance, circulation, and return of evidence, which is essential for maintaining the chain-of-custody required for evidence to be acceptable in the courts. The FBI Laboratory is accredited by the American Society of Crime Laboratory Directors/Laboratory Accreditation Board.

The FBI Seal

The FBI Laboratory provides support to the US criminal justice system at all levels. The lab provides a number of services:

- physical evidence analysis

- specialized technical and scientific support to ongoing investigations

- an automated database of DNA patterns from evidence/individuals for examination and comparison (CODIS)

- expert testimony in court

- database and network software to match and exchange images of firearms evidence from violent crimes

- specialized forensic science training, analysis, and technical assistance to crime lab personnel

- crime scene training to law enforcement personnel

CODIS (Combined DNA Index System) allows federal, state and local crime labs to exchange and compare DNA profiles electronically. This allows for easier identification of serial crimes to one another and to known criminal offenders. The Federal Convicted Offender Program is fully integrated into CODIS. The database contains more than 4,000,000 offender profiles and over 160,000 forensic profiles. As of April 2008, CODIS had been used to support nearly 69,000 investigations, including 50,000 offender hits and more than 12,000 forensics hits. Many labs, domestic and international, cooperate with the FBI Laboratory to add profiles to CODIS. This includes nearly 200 state and local laboratories in the US, as well as 40 labs in 26 countries. Over 1,200 people from 220+ labs have received CODIS training.

The FBI Laboratory has several sections, three of which we will discuss further:

- Investigative Services

- Response Services

- Research and Development Services

- Administrative and Support Services

- Quality Services

- Community Service

Investigative Services

Investigative services primarily support FBI investigations. The members of this team analyze evidence collected from crime scenes and major incidents (plane crashes, train derailments, natural disasters, etc.), as well as providing photographic services and creating models and exhibits used for investigations or in court. This group also maintains databases, such as CODIS, that are used by law enforcement to solve crimes, find missing persons, and exonerate the innocent.

FBI Evidence Response Team members plot wreckage of the I-35W bridge that collapsed August 1 in Minneapolis. The data, which collectively make up a digital representation of the fallen bridge, will be analyzed by FBI Laboratory and NTSB investigators to help determine the cause of the collapse. Photo Gallery

Response Services

This group responds to incidents that involve hazardous materials and other dangerous substances around the world. The people on these teams are extensively trained to deal with hazardous materials, explosives and other dangerous substances. This training allows them to quickly and safely contain a scene while still conducting their investigation.

Research and Development Services

This lab works to develop better forensic techniques for use by field investigators. They work with crime labs, government agencies, and academic institutions around the world to find global solutions to the problems faced by law enforcement worldwide.

Central Identification Lab

The Central Identification Laboratory is a military forensics laboratory. It is part of the Joint POW/MIA Accounting Command. The mission of CIL is to search for, recover, and identify US personnel missing from past military conflicts. CIL is accredited by the American Society of Crime Laboratory Directors/Laboratory Accreditation Board.

The three primary objectives of CIL are to:

- Recover and identify US military personnel, as well as certain civilian and allied personnel unaccounted for from World War II, the Korean War, the Vietnam War and other conflicts around the world.

- Serve as a national forensic resource.

- Advance the field of forensic science related to recovering and identifying human remains by conducting research and development.

CIL staff work to meet these objectives by recovering and identifying missing personnel using scientifically sound recovery and testing techniques. They also support humanitarian missions in support of homeland defense and national and international disasters.

Remains being repatriated at CIL in Hawai'i.

CIL forensic scientists provide forensic support to foreign governments and international organizations, provide forensic support to law enforcement and criminal investigations, and collaborate with national and international scientific and forensic organizations to further the field of forensics.

The **Forensic Science Academy** was opened by CIL at Hickam Air Force Base, Hawai'I to provide advanced forensic anthropology training. This series of five courses is designed to provide students an opportunity to learn forensic anthropology techniques.

The primary divisions in the lab are Anthropology, Archaeology, and Odontology. The **Anthropology** unit develops biological profiles of the remains recovered by the CIL team. The biological profiles allow the team to narrow down the potential list of missing individuals and to provide supporting evidence for identifications.

Forensic Archaeologists apply the principles, methods and techniques of archaeology to the legal process. These professionals recover remains of missing US service people.

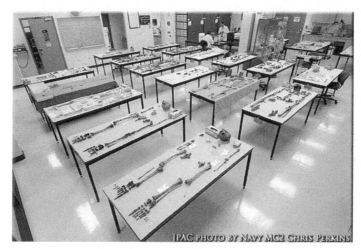
Remains in the Central Identification Lab, Hawai'i

Forensic odontology is the application of the principles, methods and techniques of dentistry to the legal process. Forensic odontology is important in identifying recovered remains.

CIL staff have developed tools to help identify individuals based on dental characteristics and eyeglass prescriptions. OdontoSearch and OptoSearch are used by the forensics community to help identify remains.

Another tool used by CIL to identify remains is family reference samples. Family members of missing military and civilian service people are able to submit DNA samples to CIL for use in identifying remains.

Opto Search

An identification tool developed by the Central ID Lab in Hawaii to determine the frequency of an eyeglass prescription in the general population. It can be useful in identifying remains if corrective lenses are found at the gravesite.

Odonto Search

An identification tool developed by the Central ID Lab in Hawaii to help identify remains using dental record comparisons.

Summary

The primary federal forensics labs in the US are the FBI Laboratory in Quantico, Virginia, and the Central Identification Laboratory at Hickam Air Force Base in Hawai'i. Both laboratories are world leaders in forensic sciences. The FBI laboratory focuses on criminal investigation. The Central Identification Laboratory recovers the remains of military personnel and works to identify them. Both laboratories cooperate with international forensics and criminal investigation agencies, as well as academic research labs, to develop better forensics techniques.

. . . .

Concept Reinforcement

1. Describe the mission of the FBI Laboratory.

2. Describe the mission of the Central ID Laboratory.

3. Explain how the databases developed by these laboratories help solve crimes and identify missing persons.

Chapter 6 – International Agencies

Chapter Objective

• Describe the role of INTERPOL in crimes that cross national borders

The History of INTERPOL

After World War 1, Europe was economically weak because of the costs of the war. This led to a massive crime wave. Johann Schober, who was the head of the 1923 Vienna police department, called for cooperation among law enforcement agencies across international borders. INTERPOL is the modern form of the law enforcement organization formed at this meeting. Interpol is an abbreviation for the International Criminal Police Organization.

The INTERPOL Seal

INTERPOL Now

Today's INTERPOL is the largest international police organization in the world. INTERPOL has 187 member nations. The mission of INTERPOL is to facilitate cross border police cooperation, and to support and assist all organizations, authorities and services with a mission to prevent or combat crime. Interpol has four official languages: Arabic, English, French and Spanish.

INTERPOL headquarters are in Lyon, France. The headquarters is the General Secretariat. The General Secretariat provides worldwide leadership and support to law enforcement agencies.

INTERPOL also has seven regional offices around the world.

- Argentina (South America)

- Cameroon (Africa)

- Côte d'Ivoire (Africa)

- El Salvador (South America)

- Kenya (Africa)

- Thailand (Southeast Asia)

- Zimbabwe (Africa)

In addition to the regional offices, INTERPOL has a representative office at the United Nations, which is located in New York City. In addition to the seven regional offices, each member country has a National Central Bureau (NCB), which is staffed by highly trained law enforcement personnel. These offices act as the primary point of contact for the General Secretariat, regional offices and other member organizations who need their assistance.

INTERPOL Core Functions

INTERPOL has four core functions: Secure global police communication services; operational data services and databases for police; operational police support services; and police training and development.

Secure global police communication services

INTERPOL manages I-24/7, which is a global police communications system used by all member countries. I-24/7 allows the law enforcement personnel in each member country to securely request, submit and access police data instantly.

Operational data services and databases for police

INTERPOL maintains a wide range of databases containing information needed by law enforcement personnel. Databases include information on known criminals, wanted persons, fingerprints, DNA profiles, stolen or lost travel documents, stolen motor vehicles, child sex abuse images and stolen works of art. In addition to maintaining and making these databases available, INTERPOL also disseminates information on international crimes using its system of seven types of international notices.

INTERPOL wanted poster

Operational police support services

INTERPOL has identified six priority crime areas and also operates a 24-hour command and control center. The six priority crime areas are corruption, drugs and organized crime, financial and high-tech crime, fugitives, public safety and terrorism, and trafficking in human beings. The command and control center supports member countries during crises, and assumes a crisis-management role during serious incidents.

Police training and development

INTERPOL provides training to the law enforcement organizations of member countries. The goal of doing this is to build the capacity of member countries to combat terrorism and international crime. This includes helping establish international standards for fighting specific crimes, as well as sharing best practices, skills and knowledge with member countries.

Activities

INTERPOL works to assist police cooperation between all countries, even if diplomatic relations do not exist between specific countries. The Universal Declaration of Human Rights and the laws of specific countries provide the framework in which action is taken by INTERPOL.

Drug trafficking is a serious problem for all of INTERPOL's member nations. The proceeds from drug sales are often used to finance other illegal activities, such as terrorism and organized crime. Drug trafficking is also closely linked to other serious crimes, such as people smuggling, organized prostitution, and travel document (passport) counterfeiting.

Organized crime is another area of interest to INTERPOL. Organized crime activities often cross international borders and include trafficking in drugs, weapons, and people, armed robbery, money laundering and counterfeiting. INTERPOL acts as a repository for information and a source of expertise for member fighting these groups.

Financial and high-Tech crimes include counterfeiting, intellectual property crimes, credit card fraud, counterfeiting, computer virus attacks and cyber terrorism. These affect everyone. INTERPOL provides resources and expertise required to help member nation law enforcement agencies solve these crimes.

Fugitive investigative services focus on apprehending wanted persons on a global level. The INTERPOL Red Notice is recognized by many countries as providing the legal support needed to arrest a person wanted by national law enforcement or international criminal tribunals.

Public safety and terrorism are a focus area for INTERPOL. They maintain records on known terrorist organization and make resources available to member organizations to protect their citizens from terrorism, including bioterrorism, firearms, attacks against civil aviation, maritime piracy, and weapons of mass destruction. The Fusion Task Force was created by INTERPOL after 9/11 to provide comprehensive tracking of terrorist organizations and support to member countries.

Trafficking in human beings is a serious issue. INTERPOL is working to end the exploitation of human beings for financial gain. Criminal smuggling of people across national borders, as well as the sexual enslavement of women and the sexual exploitation of children are both big business, generating billions of dollars of illegal revenue. This is a very destructive crime that ruins the lives of the people it touches.

Corruption is of interest to INTERPOL because it undermines social and economic stability in the areas where it occurs and has wide ranging global impact. INTERPOL has taken a global leadership role in fighting corruption. The INTERPOL Group of Experts on Corruption (IGEC) works to help law enforcement agencies around the world fight corruption. Corruption is the acting or not acting for profit or gain. Individuals can be corrupt, as can organizations, including governments and privately owned companies.

The mission of IGEC is clearly stated:

"We believe in a free and just society. To be truly just, society must embrace high standards of integrity and openly resist corruption. To this end, we joint with the community to ensure such standards and accept responsibility to fight all forms of corruption through education, prevention and effective law enforcement."

INTERPOL takes an interest in other crimes that cross international borders, including genocide, war crimes, crimes against humanity, and environmental crime.

Summary

INTERPOL is the largest international law enforcement organization in the world. As of 2009, INTERPOL has 187 member nations, all of which are supported by its seven regional offices and National Central Bureaus. INTERPOL has four core service areas and six types of crimes they focus on. The experts at INTERPOL work with regional and national law enforcement agencies to solve crimes that cross international borders.

. . . .

Concept Reinforcement

1. Describe the mission of INTERPOL.

2. Explain why INTERPOL was established.

3. Discuss the importance of collaborating to solve crimes across international borders.

Chapter 7 – Crime Scene Processing

Chapter Objective

- Describe a crime scene and how it is processed

The Crime Scene

A crime scene is the place a crime was committed. Regardless of how careful a criminal is, he is likely to leave evidence of some sort that a careful crime scene investigator will find and which can be used to solve the crime. Most crimes are committed in the heat of the moment, which usually results in a messy crime scene. A criminal will leave behind evidence in the form of fingerprints, hair, fibers, blood stains, noise, and anything else that is involved in the crime. The primary crime scene is where the crime actually occurs. Secondary crime scenes are related to the crime, but are not where the crime took place.

A crime scene during an investigation
Photo courtesy US Army CID

What happens at a crime scene?

Arrival at the crime scene

The first people to arrive at a crime scene are usually the police. Once they determine a crime has occurred, they follow a strict set of procedures to secure the crime scene, collect and log the evidence, transport the evidence and ensure the chain of custody. These protocols are designed to protect the officer and others at the scene; ensure that the evidence is kept safe from contamination, loss and damage; and document everything at the crime scene, as well as everything that occurs at the crime scene.

It is important for the officers who arrive at the scene to ensure that anyone who is there when the police arrive is detained for questioning and kept away from the crime scene. Sometimes the person who calls in a crime is actually the person who committed the crime. The perpetrator may try to deflect suspicion by reporting the crime and may also try to tamper with evidence if allowed to touch anything at the crime scene itself.

> **Crime Scene Processing Steps**
>
> Determine that a crime scene exists.
>
> Secure crime scene.
>
> Process crime scene, including identifying and collecting evidence.
>
> Document crime scene.
>
> Reconstruct the crime.

Processing the crime scene

The crime scene may actually be hard to determine. It can be a small area or a large area, depending upon the crime. A crime scene includes, at a minimum, the exact location of the crime, any entries or exits, and the locations of all key pieces of evidence. A crime scene is secured using crime scene tape, barricades, vehicles, and people. The tools used to secure the crime scene depend upon the crime scene itself. It is very important to limit who has access to the crime scene once it is identified and secured. A security log is used to track who goes into the crime scene. This log is used to limit the number of people who must be ruled out as suspects when evidence is being examined. Investigators may accidentally leave some sort of trace evidence at the crime scene while they are investigating it, but that evidence is not usually relevant to the prosecution of the case itself. For example, an investigator may shed a hair or leave a shoe print at the crime scene that will need to be excluded from the analysis. Once the crime scene is secured, the crime scene investigator (CSI) begins with a walk through examination of the crime scene to figure out how to best process the scene and collect the evidence it holds.

Documenting the scene

It is critical to thoroughly document a crime scene. The scene is documented using photography, sketches, and notes. A designated note-taker is responsible for documenting the crime scene, including all activities at the scene. The note taker may use different tools to document the scene, including note pads and tape recorders. In addition to having a text record of the crime scene, it is important to also make a visual record of the scene.

Crime scene sketches are used to document the location of different items related to the crime. These sketches show the relationships between objects, the position and location of any bodies, as well as the distances between objects. These sketches usually have a legend that has a description of the key objects in the scene. It is important that the sketches are accurate even if they are rough. This means that measurements must be accurate, but the sketch of the object can be rough.

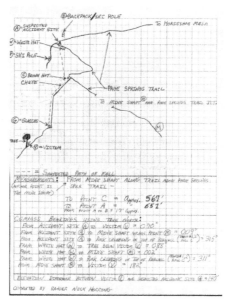

Sketch of the crime scene of a possible double murder/suicide.
Image courtesy of the FBI.

Photographers document the scene, witnesses and victims of a crime. The photographer documents the scene as soon as possible to capture the crime scene before it is altered by the actions of the investigators. Photographers are careful to use a point of reference, such as a measuring device, to help the investigators maintain a proper perspective when viewing the picture. Videotape is sometimes used to document a crime scene. Video has the added benefit of making voice recordings, as well.

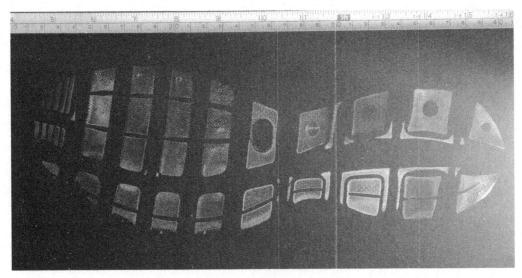

An example of a photograph using a frame of reference (the measuring tape).
Image courtesy of Zalman992

Reconstructing the crime

Once the crime scene is documented, the CSI will try to reconstruct the crime itself by looking at the evidence at the scene. Footprints, fingerprints, tool marks, disturbed furniture, blood stains, bullets and a number of other types of evidence will give the CSI clues about what happened. As the CSI is forming the theory, he is also testing it against the evidence to make sure it makes sense. This process will also help the CSI determine if the crime scene is real or staged. Criminals will stage crime scenes to point the police to another suspect. A person who decides to stage a burglary, for example, might do a number of things to make the police think a robbery actually occurred. These things include removing the "stolen" things from the property and staging a break-in by breaking glass or leaving tool marks at an entry point.

Summary

The first people who arrive at a crime scene have the critical job of determining whether a crime scene exists, securing the crime scene, and detaining anyone at the crime scene for questioning. Once the crime scene is secured, the crime scene investigators document and investigate the crime scene. Documentation is done in a number of ways. Note taking is critical for documenting everything that occurs at the scene. Photography and crime scene sketches are used to create visual documentation of the scene. Video may be used, as well, for crime scene documentation. Once the scene is documented, the CSI will recreate the scene and test theories against the evidence at the scene.

Concept Reinforcement

1. Explain the role of the first law enforcement person to arrive at a crime scene.

2. List and describe the three primary forms of crime scene documentation.

3. Explain the importance of a frame of reference in crime scene images.

Chapter 8 – The Locard Exchange Principle

Chapter Objective

- Describe the importance of the Locard Exchange Principle

The Locard Exchange Principle

The **Locard Exchange Principle** describes the exchange of materials that occurs every time you make contact with another person, place or object. This evidence is also called **trace evidence**. It allows investigators to trace where the criminal was and often in what order, based on how the exchanges took place.

Dr. Edmond Locard, a French police officer, was the first person to notice this exchange of materials. This observation forms the basis of modern forensic investigations. Dr. Locard noticed that every time there is contact between two items, there is an exchange of materials. This can be fiber, hair, dirt, body fluids, blood, or anything else that can be transferred between objects. Trace evidence occurs in small, measurable amounts. Trace evidence is not always easily seen, but can be found with careful investigation. As long as the evidence is measurable, it can be used in an investigation.

A US Park Police Identification Officer analyzing evidence.
Image courtesy US Federal Government

Edmond Locard

Who was Edmond Locard? He was a medical examiner who also directed the very first crime lab ever established. This lab was opened in 1910 and located in Lyon, France. Dr. Locard's observation that every contact leaves trace evidence of the contact was useful to the French Secret Service during World War I. Dr. Locard was able to establish where prisoners and soldiers died based on the stains he found on their uniforms.

> The Locard Exchange Principle
>
> Contact between two items will always result in an exchange between the items. This is the basis of trace evidence collection at a crime scene.

> Locard quote:
>
> "It is impossible for a criminal to act, especially considering the intensity of a crime, without leaving traces of this presence."

Trace Evidence

Trace evidence is any material related to a crime scene. Trace evidence may be left at a crime scene. It may also be removed from a crime scene. Trace evidence is usually the result of contact between two surfaces. One reason it is so important to secure a crime scene is to protect trace evidence. This is also important to prevent the deposit of more trace evidence by police officers and others at the crime scene.

Trace evidence may be nearly invisible, but can be critical to solving a crime. Because trace evidence can be so small, the crime scene must be thoroughly investigated by the CSIs, who find, collect, document and transport the evidence following protocols that maintain the chain of custody required to use the evidence in a trial.

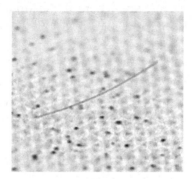

A single hair, found on a garment while examining it for visible gunshot residues.
Image courtesy of US Department of Justice

Types of Trace Evidence

There are many types of trace evidence. These include bone fragments, teeth, hair, gunshot residue, skin, fingerprints, fibers, paper, glass, paint chips, soils, metals, plant materials, and animal fur. There may be others. It just depends on the crime scene.

Bone fragments and teeth may provide information about the weapons used in the crime, the type of bullet used and its trajectory, the identity of the person (if DNA is present), as well as a general biological profile of the person if enough information is available.

Hair and skin can be used to help identify individual people and place them at a specific crime scene. Sometimes the identification is made based on DNA. Hair samples can be matched based on the morphology (physical characteristics) of the hair. Hair from a person can often be matched to a trace evidence by microscopic analysis. If the hair sample has a root or piece of skin attached to it, DNA analysis is performed to identify the individual belonging to the hair. Animal fur can be used in the same way. Animal hair transfers to clothing very easily, as anyone who has petted a cat knows. Animal fur can be matched to the animal that shed the fur, helping narrow down the crime scene.

Fingerprints are unique to each individual, making them useful for identifying criminals. Fingerprints occur because the oils on our hands and the ridges on our fingertips leave a unique pattern on anything we touch. Your fingerprint is different than you best friend's, making it easy to determine who touched what.

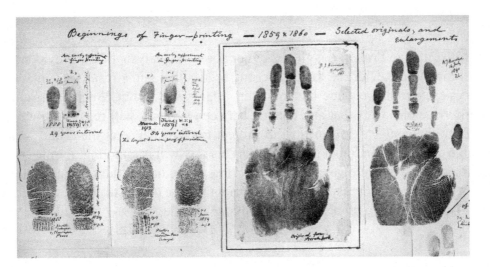

The first fingerprints taken in 1859 or 1860 by William James Herschel. Notice that he took prints of the entire hand, as well. Each person's palm makes a unique palm print, which can also be helpful in identifying criminals.

Fibers from clothing and other fabrics are often left at crime scenes. Remember that Locard's Theory relates to trace evidence resulting from contact between two surfaces. Most fabrics will shed fibers when they are rubbed against something else, leaving trace evidence at the scene. Since many crimes are messy, there is likely to fiber evidence that can be used to figure out what happened.

Glass, paint chips, soils and metals are valuable trace evidence to CSIs. Each brand of glass, paint, and metal has a unique chemical signature. This chemical makeup can be used to trace the material back to a manufacturer or to match it to other materials at the crime scene or a suspect's home, car, or office. Soils also have unique characteristics. These are based on the composition of soil in different places. The geology of the soil's source will provide one set of clues. Is the soil full of a particular mineral? Is the texture of the soil coarse or fine? Clay, loam or sand? If the soil comes from a site that has been contaminated by something (a factory, dump site, etc.), the contaminants will help the investigators narrow down the original location of the soil.

Botanical materials can also provide clues to the location of a crime. Plants grow in different areas. Sometimes a plant grows in only a very small, specific area because of the unique requirements of the plant for survival. This will help the investigator narrow down the location of the crime.

Gunshot residue tells the CSI if the fabric or other evidence were near a weapon when it was fired. The amount of gunshot residue (GSR) and the pattern of GSR may be useful in determining the relative location of the gun to the evidence.

Summary

The Locard Exchange Principle is the basis for forensic analysis of trace evidence. Trace evidence is the minute evidence found at crime scenes that is the result of contact between two surfaces. Examples include hair transfer, fingerprints, paint chips, soil samples, etc. The Locard Principle states that any contact between surfaces will result in trace evidence resulting from the contact. It is critical to protect trace evidence at the crime scene so the CSIs are able to collect it before it is disturbed. This is why it is important for the crime scene to be secured and no one allowed to enter the crime scene before the CSIs collect evidence. Everyone who enters a crime scene, whether or not they are part of the crime, will leave trace evidence. Trace evidence can be critical to solving a crime.

. . . .

Concept Reinforcement

1. State the Locard Exchange Principle.

2. Explain the importance of protecting the crime scene in terms of trace evidence.

3. List three types of trace evidence.

Chapter 9 – Evidence Collection

Chapter Objective

- Describe the proper way to collect evidence and maintain the chain of custody

Evidence Collection

Finding Evidence

The first step in collecting evidence from a crime scene is actually finding the evidence. Some evidence is obvious and other evidence may not be visible to the unaided human eye. This means that the search for evidence must conducted in a logical and orderly manner. The techniques used to find evidence will depend upon the crime scene. A small crime scene will be searched differently than a large crime scene. The type of crime also determines the way the crime scene is searched. If the crime is a burglary, safes, jewelry boxes, and other areas where valuable are stored will be key sources of evidence. If the crime is a violent crime, such as a murder or assault, the investigators may focus on the location of the body or assault victim, as well as the entries and exits to the crime scene.

Evidence searches are usually done following a geometrical pattern. The size and type of crime scene will determine which search pattern is used. It may be that multiple search patterns are used, depending upon the scene. The ultimate goal is to search every square inch of the crime scene for evidence.

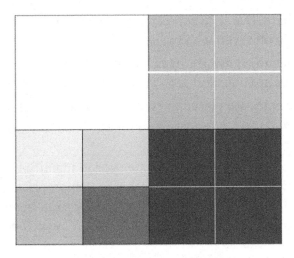

A quadrant search pattern. This is also known as a zone search pattern. Each color represents a search area. The bottom left quadrant is further divided into four unique search areas. Searches are also conducted in spiral, linear or grid patterns, depending upon the scene and the crime.
Image courtesy Susan Carlson

Collecting the Evidence

Evidence collection is a critical part of solving a crime. CSIs follow very specific protocols for collecting, documenting, protecting and transporting evidence. These protocols are necessary for both protecting the integrity of the evidence and for maintaining the chain of custody of the evidence. **Chain of custody** is a record of who has had control of the evidence and everything that was done to the evidence. If the chain of custody is broken, the evidence may not be admissible in court. If a critical piece of evidence is compromised (damaged evidence, broken chain of custody), the prosecutor will not be able to use the evidence in the trial. This may result in the accused going free, whether or not he or she is guilty of the crime.

The first evidence collected is usually the most fragile evidence. This also includes evidence that his likely to be lost, damaged or contaminated. Trace evidence (blood, fibers, fingerprints, hair, shoeprints, tire tracks) is a prime example of the evidence first collected at a crime scene. Outdoor crime scenes are more susceptible to loss, damage or contamination of evidence because it is difficult to secure the evidence from the elements. Rain and wind will damage or erase evidence quickly.

Evidence collection techniques

Evidence Search Patterns:

Grid

Linear

Quadrant/ Zone

Spiral

Type of Evidence	Technique used to gather evidence.
Fingerprints	Photographed, then lifted or transferred to a material that can be moved to the crime lab.
Tool marks, shoe prints, tire impressions	Photographed, then lifted or cast.
Fibers and hair	Alternative light sources are used to identify evidence, which is then retrieved with tweezers and placed in an evidence container.
Carpets and furniture	Vacuumed using a fresh vacuum cleaner bag for each area. The bags are transported to the crime lab for further analysis.
Plant, soil, glass, metal, and other solid samples	Samples are placed in evidence containers for analysis at the crime lab.
Bodily fluids	Alternative light sources are used to identify bodily fluids, which are then collected using techniques appropriate to the surface they are found on. Fabrics are bagged for examination. Liquid samples are put into rigid, unbreakable, sterile, sealed containers.

Collecting trace evidence from a rug.
Image courtesy of FBI.

Evidence packaging techniques

Each piece of evidence is packaged separately to prevent cross-contamination and damage to the samples.

Type of Evidence	Packaging technique
Dry trace evidence	Placed in druggist's folds, which are small folded papers. This type of evidence may also be placed in paper or plastic bags, envelopes, canisters, or plastic pill bottles, depending upon the type of evidence.
Documents	Sealed in plastic bags for transport to the lab.
Liquid evidence	Placed in solid, airtight, unbreakable, sealed containers.
Solid evidence that may contain volatile evidence	Placed in solid, airtight, unbreakable, sealed containers to retain the volatile evidence. Clean paint cans and tightly sealed jars work well for solid evidence.
Moist or wet biological evidence	Place in non-airtight containers so the evidence is able to dry before mold, mildew or bacterial can damage the evidence. Clothing or other large pieces of fiber evidence may be hung to dry thoroughly before it is packaged in a sealed container.
Tool marks and bullet holes.	Processed at the scene or the item with the tool mark is removed from the scene for analysis at the crime lab.

Control Samples

Control samples are samples taken from a known source. They are used to exclude people as suspects, as well as to confirm the source of evidence. The evidence source may be the suspect, victim, or items at the crime scene. Control samples may also be things that are identical to materials on which evidence was found. For example, a piece of fabric from a crime scene can be compared to an identical piece of fabric that was not exposed to the crime scene to determine if there are any compounds related to the crime on the fabric. This is often used in arson cases. Arsonists usually use an accelerant of some sort to start the fire. There will be traces of the accelerant on or in the carpet, wood, or fabrics at the fire scene. Comparison with undamaged samples helps narrow down the accelerant used to start the fire.

Chain of Custody

The chain of custody is a continuous record of the evidence. The record shows that the evidence was controlled (kept safe and secure) during transport from the crime scene to the lab and then to the courtroom. If the chain of custody is broken, the evidence may not be admissible in court.

The chain of custody includes evidence marks for identification of certain types of evidence; evidence bags with the case number, name and description of the item, name and initials of the investigator who found it, the names of people who witnessed the discovery and recovery of the evidence; and the date, time and location of the find. Samples that require special handling, such as blood, may have multiple levels of marking because each container (test tube, plastic evidence bag, etc) must be marked.

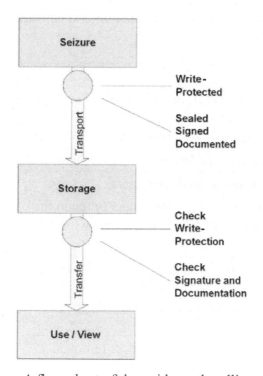

A flow chart of the evidence handling protocol followed to maintain the chain of custody of digital images. Image courtesy of the Federal Bureau of Investigation

Evidence is handled by several different groups during the investigation of a crime. The police officer or CSI who finds the evidence is responsible for marking and bagging it. This protects the evidence from contamination and maintains the chain of custody. The lab tech signs for the evidence when it arrives at the crime lab for analysis. Once the evidence is evaluated, the lab tech turns the evidence over to the police evidence custodian, who signs for it and makes sure it is properly stored. The prosecuting attorney will then sign the evidence out for use in the trial. All transfers of the evidence must be properly documented in order for it to be admissible during the trial.

Summary

Evidence collection is a crucial part of processing every crime scene. CSIs follow specific protocols to collecting, protecting, handling and transporting evidence from the crime scene to the laboratory. If the evidence is damaged or the chain of custody is broken, the evidence will not be admissible in court. This may allow the suspect to go free even if the inadmissible evidence proves the suspect's guilt.

Concept Reinforcement

1. Explain why fragile evidence is collected first.

2. State why each piece of evidence is packaged separately.

3. Describe the importance of the chain of custody.

Chapter 10 – Physical Collection

Chapter Objectives

- Explain the types of physical evidence that can be collected from a crime scene

Types of Physical Evidence

Physical evidence is any evidence that is non-living or inorganic.

A list of physical evidence includes:

- Fingerprints
- Shoe impressions
- Tire impressions
- Tools and tool marks
- Fibers
- Paint
- Drugs
- Firearms
- Bullets and shell casings
- Documents
- Explosives
- Distilled fire accelerants
- Soil and minerals
- Glass
- Rope and tape
- Fingerprints

Fingerprints are a type of individual evidence. Individual evidence narrows identification down to a single person. Each person has a unique fingerprint, which makes fingerprints individual evidence. A fingerprint is a form of trace evidence formed when a person touches a surface, depositing the oils from the and in the form of the ridges on the tip of the finger.

The FBI wanted poster for Clyde Barrow with his fingerprints.
Image courtesy of the Federal Bureau of Investigation

Shoe impressions

Shoes make unique impressions. Each person walks differently, which results in different wear patterns on the soles and heels of the shoe. The way a person walks also affects the depth of a shoe print, as do size and weight. Shoes can be matched to shoe impressions, helping to narrow down the suspects.

Tire impressions

Tires make unique impressions based on the way the car drives. If a car is out of alignment, for example, the tires will wear unevenly. Different tire brands have different tread patterns, which are used to narrow down the type of tire, and possibly vehicle, that made the tire impressions. Tire impressions can be matched to the tire that made the impression.

A test tire tread impression
Courtesy Federal Bureau of Investigation

Tools and Tool Marks

Each tool leaves unique marks on whatever it touches. A pry bar makes specific tool marks that are different than the marks made by a hammer. A person must apply a tool to a surface in order to use it. A pry bar is used to pry something open, which will leave tool marks on the door or window it is used to open. There may even be paint transfer from the surface to the tool.

Fibers

Wool fiber

Anything made of fabric will shed fibers. Clothing, carpeting, curtains, blankets, sheets, and anything else made of fibrous material will shed fibers. Again, fibers are trace evidence that are usually left at a crime scene because of contact with something. Different types of fibers have unique characteristics. Cotton fiber will look different under a microscope than wool, for example. Fibers may also occur in specific blends of fibers (cotton/polyester, for example) or have a specific chemical makeup (carpet fibers). These characteristics are useful in narrowing down the suspect pool.

Paint

Each paint has a different chemical structure, which makes it possible to identify the paint by brand and color. Paint transfer can be used to match evidence from a car crash, for example. If it is a hit and run, the paint transfer from one car to the other may provide enough clues to find the suspect based on the type of cars with that paint.

Drugs

Each batch of drugs has a unique chemical signature. Do you see a pattern here yet? Chemistry is very important in analyzing the evidence from crime scenes. The components of a drug may help the police track down a specific drug dealer. Chemistry is also used to prove that the suspected drug is actually a drug, as well as the type of drug. Some drugs look similar, so chemistry is used to identify the specific compound. Cocaine has a different chemical signature than heroin, for example.

Seized drugs.
Image courtesy of US State Department

Firearms, bullets and shell casings

Firearms have different physical characteristics that can be used to identify the make and model of a weapon. Firearms also make distinctive marks on bullets and shell casings. These distinctive marks are used to match bullets and shell casings to the weapons that fired them. They are also used to match bullets and shell casings to other crime scenes in which a weapon may have been used.

Documents

Documents are often critical evidence in a case. Documents may prove a connection between the suspect and the crime, or may be evidence of fraud or counterfeiting activity. Document examination techniques allow investigators to confirm the authenticity of documents. These techniques are also used to identify forgeries, determine the how the document was created (typewritten, laser printed, etc), define the type of ink used, and so on.

Explosives

Explosives are separated into two categories: high explosive and low explosives. High explosives create a pressure wave that may move as fast as 8,500 meters per second. Low explosives create a pressure wave that moves less than 1,000 meters per second.

Low explosives include black powder and smokeless gunpowder. Low explosives are easy to make with commonly available items. An example is combining sugar and potassium chloride. High explosives are further divided into two categories: initiating explosives and non-initiating explosives. As their names infer, an initiating explosive is very sensitive to heat, friction or mechanical shock. If the explosive is exposed to any of these forces, the explosive will ignite. An example of an initiating explosive is mercury fulminate. Non-initiating explosives are less sensitive to heat, friction and mechanical shock. Non-initiating explosives are used by military and commercial groups and include dynamite and TNT. Fertilizer contains ammonium nitrate, which can be used to make a non-initiating explosive.

> **Mercury Fulminate**
> An explosive that is highly sensitive to friction and shock. A primary use is in blasting caps.

Distilled Fire Accelerants

Most arsonists use an accelerant to start the fire and make it burn quickly. Accelerants include alcohol, lighter fluid, and other flammable liquids that help the fire burn hot and spread quickly. These accelerants leave a distinctive chemical signature at the fire scene. A crime lab is able to narrow down the type of accelerant by analyzing the evidence at the arson scene.

Soil and minerals

Soil from different places has different characteristics. These include the texture of the soil: loamy, sandy, clay, gravel. They also include the mineral composition of the soil. Soil near chemical dump sites or from specific places may have additional characteristics that tie it specifically to that site. For example, soil near an airport is likely to have jet fuel in it. This piece of information would narrow down the search to areas in or near airports.

Glass

Glass, like other physical evidence, has unique physical and chemical characteristics. The color and texture of glass, as well as the type of glass can help the CSI narrow down the source of the glass. Safety glass, for example, is different from the glass used in a house window or water glass. It may even be possible to narrow the glass down to a specific location or manufacturer.

Rope and tape

Rope and tape are often used to restrain victims of crimes or to wrap objects that are used crime. Rope and tape are made from different materials. Rope can be made of hemp, nylon, or a number of other materials. Rope also has different physical characteristics, depending upon how it is made. Some rope is braided. Other rope is twisted. These characteristics can be used to match specific types of rope to a wound or rub mark on evidence. Similarly, tape can be made from a number of different materials. Some characteristics of tape are the adhesive used on the tape, the width of the tape, and the tear patterns on the ends of the tape.

This adhesive tape is evidence from the Brinks Robberies of 1950.
Image courtesy Federal Bureau of Investigation

Summary

A wide range of physical evidence can be collected from a crime scene. Much of it is subjected to chemical analysis to understand the composition of the evidence. This information can be used to trace the source of evidence or match it to other evidence from the crime scene or to other crime scenes.

. . . .

Concept Reinforcement

1. Define physical evidence.

2. Explain why chemistry is important in analyzing physical evidence.

3. Describe how the patterns from rope or tape can be used to solve crimes.

Chapter 11 – Crime Scene Reconstruction

Chapter Objective

- Explain the importance of crime scene reconstruction

What is crime scene reconstruction?

Crime scene reconstruction refers to the use of scientific methods, deductive reasoning, and physical evidence to figure out the events that led up to the crime or occurred during the crime. Crime scene investigators and other forensic professionals use their understanding of physical evidence to recreate the events of a crime.

Crime scene reconstruction begins after the investigator does the first walk through of the crime scene. As the CSI walks through the scene, she gains an understanding of the types of physical evidence at the scene, the physical relationships between the different pieces of evidence, and potentially an idea of the order in which events took place. The investigator develops a theory of the crime, which she constantly tests against the evidence. If the evidence does not support the theory, the theory is adapted based on the evidence available. For example, if a crime appears to involve a break-in, key evidence will be found at the point of entry. Tool marks, broken glass, shoe prints, and other evidence can be used to help understand how the person gained entry. It could also be that someone tried to make it look like a burglary, when in fact it was not. This is called a staged crime scene.

The evidence found at a crime scene is also used to support or refute the testimony given by witnesses and the accused. Some types of physical evidence are commonly found at crime scenes and used for reconstructing the scene. These include shoe prints (movement of the perpetrator), fingerprints (helps identify things the perpetrator touched), tool marks (points of entry or attempts to get into locked rooms, safes, cabinets, etc), blood spatter and bullet trajectories can be used to show the relationship between perpetrator(s) and victim(s).

Categories and Types of Crime Scene Reconstruction

There are three categories of physical crime scene reconstruction. These include specific incident reconstruction, specific event reconstruction, and specific physical evidence reconstruction. Sometimes it is possible to do a complete crime scene reconstruction. Other times it may be possible to do only a partial reconstruction. Additionally, some types of crime scenes are easier to reconstruct than others. Car accidents are relatively easy to recreate because of the amount of evidence left by the accident itself. The car(s) will be damaged, the road will have skid marks, glass will be broken and paint transferred. This evidence, combined with a scientific analysis based on the laws of physics and other disciplines, allows the CSI to recreate the accident scene fairly accurately.

Specific incident reconstruction refers to recreating the events of a crime. For example, understanding what happened during a kidnapping, murder, car accident, burglary, bombing, etc.

A US Army CID crime scene investigator
Image courtesy US Army

Specific event reconstruction can be more difficult because this requires finding evidence of how people moved through a scene. There is often evidence of people being at several different locations within a crime scene, but it is not often possible to determine how the people moved from point to point. It is not possible to recreate the gestures, body language, facial expressions and conversations that occur at a crime scene.

Specific physical evidence reconstruction involves the use of specific pieces of physical evidence to recreate some part of the crime. A well-known example is ballistics, which allows CSIs to determine the type of gun, match a bullet to a gun, and possibly even the direction the shot was fired.

Types of reconstructions

Many types of evidence reconstruction are used when analyzing evidence and trying to solve a crime. Different reconstructions result in different types of evidence.

Type of Reconstruction	Information gained
Blood and Blood Stain Pattern Analysis	Identity of a person. Position and location of the victim or perpetrator. Movement of people within the crime scene. Minimum number of blows struck and the type of weapon used. Whether the scene is staged or secondary (the initial crime was committed elsewhere).

Documents	Recovery of information from reassembled papers that were torn or shredded to hide evidence.
	Recovery of erased or obliterated writing.
	Specific information about the ink and paper used.
Firearms	Bullet trajectory
	Distance
	Position and location of the shooter and victim.
	Sequence and direction of shots fired.
	Whether the wound is self-inflicted or not.
	Identification of the weapon and potential matches to weapons used in other crimes.
Functional Evidence	Is the gun empty?
	Does the vehicle work properly?
	Were appliances at the scene left on?
	Are the door and window locks secure?
	Is the security system armed or not?
Glass	Direction of the break
	Sequence and direction of gunshots
	Type of tool used to break the glass.
Impression Evidence	Identity of victim or criminal (fingerprints, shoe prints)
	Type of vehicle used and vehicle position and direction of travel (tire tracks)
	Identification of where the victim and criminal were in the crime scene location, and possible how an object was held.
	Shoe prints might provide information on the direction of movement.
Ligature	What was used to choke the person?
	Whether this type of ligature was used in other cases, leading to a potential link for serial cases.
	The type of ligature may provide clues about the occupation or interests of the criminal.

Pathology	Manner of death (homicide, suicide, natural, accidental)
	Approximate time of death
	Cause of death, including the weapon used.
	Approximate time before death the victim was incapacitated from wounds.
	Timing of the injuries (pre- or post-mortem)
	Age, identity, and other attributes of the victim.
	Whether or not sexual assault occurred, and in what manner.
	Whether wounds are self-inflicted or not.
Physical Match	Bombs
	Glass objects (lamps, mirrors, windows, etc.)
	Aircraft that crashed or exploded.
Relational/Positional Evidence	Blood drops and spatter.
	Physical locations of objects and their condition.
	Bodily fluids can be used to place people at crime scenes.
Trace Evidence	Bullet trajectory
	Place criminal and/or victim at the scene (hair, saliva, blood, other bodily fluids). It may also narrow down where a person was within a crime scene.
	Describes the environment of an unknown crime scene.
Vehicle	Positions
	Speeds
	Sequence of accident events

What information is needed to reconstruct a crime scene?

A crime scene reconstruction relies on information from a number of sources. The physical evidence found at the scene is critical, as is any information provided by witnesses and reports of analyses done by experts. This information should be collected during the initial documentation of the crime scene. All photos, documents, sketches, notes, reports, measurements, autopsy protocol, and items of evidence are necessary to accurately recreate the crime scene.

There are several steps that culminate in a reconstructed crime scene. These include evidence recognition, documentation, collection, and evaluation, as well as hypothesis development and testing, and finally reconstruction.

Evidence collection is essential to crime scene reconstruction. If the CSI misses pieces of evidence, it may affect the theory of the crime as well as the police department's ability to solve the crime. Evidence recognition, documentation and collection are the base upon which the reconstruction is built.

Evidence evaluation occurs after the laboratory has tested the evidence. Witness statements are compared to the physical evidence. Inconsistencies between witness statements and the physical evidence may weaken the hypothesis of the crime. The hypothesis of the crime is a theory, supported by the evidence, of how the crime was committed. Hypothesis testing is further examination of the evidence compared to the theory of the crime. The hypothesis may be refined based on this testing.

Consider a staged crime scene. In this example, the staged crime is a kidnapping. In this scenario, the "kidnapper" pretended to kidnap her child for ransom. The police will look for inconsistencies in the evidence. Does the physical evidence from the scene match the witness statement? In this case, it does not, because the kidnapper forgot that the alarm company keeps records of when the house security alarm is armed and when it is not. The system also tracks who arms and disarms the system each time. A kidnapper would probably not have the alarm code. Therefore, it makes sense that a kidnapping is likely to trip an alarm as it is occurring. The lack of an alarm will cause the investigators to dig more deeply into the details of the case until the theory of the crime fits facts presented by the evidence.

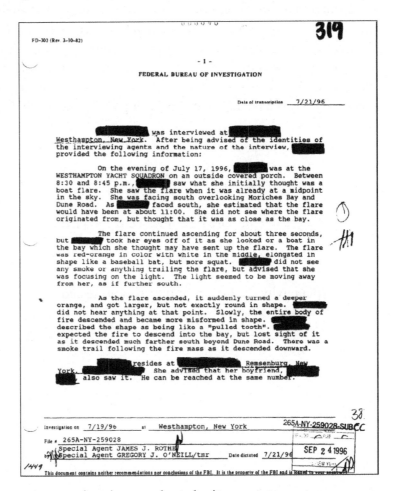

A page showing a redacted witness statement summary from the FBI investigation of an airplane crash.
Image courtesy of the Federal Bureau of Investigation

The reconstruction of the crime is a report of the results of the analysis. The report states how likely the evidence is to prove the events of the crime.

This reporting is usually done in four levels:

- The crime can be shown to have occurred in a given manner

- The crime can be shown to be likely to have occurred in a given manner

- The crime can be shown to be unlikely to have occurred in a given manner

- The crime can be shown not to have occurred in a given manner.

Summary

Crime scene reconstruction is a complex process that results in a report (the reconstruction) that describes the ability of the evidence to support the theory of the crime. Every activity performed in documenting the scene and collecting and analyzing the evidence is critical to the reconstruction process. All evidence is essential to crime scene reconstruction. Once the evidence is collected and analyzed, the theory of the crime is tested against the evidence. If the theory does not fit the evidence, the theory is adapted until it does. The result of the analysis is the reconstruction of the crime, including an assessment of how likely the crime can be shown to have occurred according to the theory of the crime.

Concept Reinforcement

1. Describe the purpose of crime scene reconstruction.

2. List the three categories of physical crime scene reconstruction.

3. Explain why the theory of the crime is tested against the evidence.

Chapter 12 – Physical Evidence Analysis

Chapter Objective

- Explain the importance of physical evidence analysis and objectivity

Physical Evidence Analysis

Physical evidence analysis is the analysis of all physical evidence found at a crime scene. This may include fingerprint analysis, shoe print or tire tread impression analysis, ballistics, and many other things that may be involved in a crime scene. Items used to cause blunt force trauma must be matched to the wound. Bullets can be matched to a weapon. They may also be used to determine the trajectory of the bullet and the locations of the shooter and victim. Stab wound characteristics can be matched to a specific type of blade used based on the length, depth and wound characteristics. Other physical evidence may be used to do bite mark analysis, match shoe or tire mark casts to specific shoes or vehicles. Blood spatter is used to understand the location of the victim and criminal. Physical evidence is essential to solving crimes.

Objectivity is very important to solving crime. Evidence may appear to show one scenario, especially at a staged crime scene. A good CSI team will discover the truth of the matter by remaining objective when collecting, documenting and analyzing evidence. This requires a thorough understanding of the possible relationships between data, as well as what the relationships say about how the crime occurred.

Objectivity is also essential to providing the police with good leads for solving the crime. Objective analysis of the evidence may lead to changes in the theory of the crime. If the theory of the crime is refined based on objective analysis, the police will have better leads they can follow to arrest the right person. Another benefit to objective analysis of the physical evidence is that it will be admissible in court and help the prosecutor win the case.

A forensic case issue checklist is used to ensure that all of the necessary steps, documentation and procedures are followed when handling and analyzing evidence from a crime scene. A sample list includes the following:

- Evidence collection

  - Item Description

  - Item Packaging

  - Item Labeling

  - Photographs

  - Diagrams of location site

- Evidence Transportation and Storage

    - From Scene

    - To and from Storage

    - To and from Laboratory

    - To and from Court

    - Back to storage or laboratory

    - Elsewhere

- At Laboratory

    - Intake

    - Lab Number

    - Packaging (compare with original)

    - Description of Evidence Item

        - Weight

        - Diagrams

        - Photos

    - Manipulation of evidence item

        - Cutting

        - Staining

    - Testing

        - Quality of documentation

        - Description of test

        - Preparation of solutions or other testing material

        - Procedures followed

        - Positive and Negative Controls

        - Amount of evidence used

        - Preliminary results

        - Peer review

        - Repackaging

- Reporting

    - Interpretation

    - Specificity

- Accuracy

Discoverable material is information that the defense attorney is allowed to request from the crime lab. Discoverable material includes lab protocols, quality control programs and documentation, technician qualification, case specific material, and other relevant material. Any of this information can be used against the prosecution to weaken the case against the accused. It may also result in the accused taking a deal to avoid the cost and stress of a trial with an assured outcome of guilty. Because discoverable material is so important to the prosecution of the case, everything included in the material must be accurate and above criticism by the defense.

Evidence bags in an FBI evidence storage facility
Image courtesy of the FBI.

A sample list of discoverable material is below:

- Laboratory Specific Material

    - Laboratory Quality Control Manual

    - Laboratory Quality Assurance Manual

    - Laboratory Protocol Manual (overall)

    - Laboratory Protocol Manual (for each test performed)

    - Laboratory Procedures Manual (sometimes the same as the Protocol Manual)

    - Laboratory Proficiency test results

- Technician Specific Material

    - Technician's CV

    - Technician's Proficiency test results for the lab technician

    - Data underlying laboratory technician's proficiency tests

- Case Specific Material

  - Technician's Benchnotes

  - Sketches, Diagrams, and Charts

  - Photographs of Evidence

  - Photographs of gels

  - Positive and Negative controls

  - Validation studies

  - Documents relied upon or referred to by technician in reaching conclusions

- Other Material

  - Membership requirements for technician's associations and organizations

  - Testing protocol for any certifying associations and organizations

  - Code of Ethics for any associations and organizations

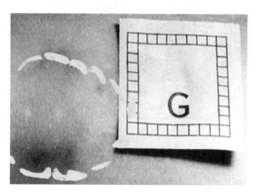

Photographic bite mark evidence.
Image courtesy of the FBI.

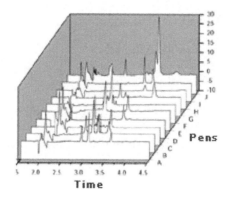

A graph of ink analysis showing a comparison of several different pens.

Summary

Physical evidence analysis is crucial to the convicting the correct person of a crime. Evidence identification, collection, transport, and analysis must be completely documented. Analysis must be completely objective. Evidence analysis provides the leads the police follow to identify the criminal(s) in a specific case. The same evidence supports the prosecution's case against the accused. A forensics case issue checklist is one way of making sure that every necessary step is taken and documented appropriately. A discoverable materials checklist is a list of documents that a defense attorney is allowed to request while preparing for trial. Any weaknesses in the discoverable material are likely to damage the prosecution's case. Therefore, it is important to make sure that everything is complete, accurate and appropriate.

Concept Reinforcement

1. Give two reasons that physical evidence analysis is important.

2. Explain why objectivity is important.

3. Describe why discoverable material checklists and forensic case issue checklists can be useful.

Chapter 13 – The Criminal Trial

Chapter Objective

- Discuss the elements of a criminal trial

What is a criminal trial?

A criminal trial is the process by which a person accused of a crime is tried in front of a jury of his peers. The sixth amendment to the US Constitution guarantees the accused the right of a speedy and public trial by a jury of peers of the accused. It is thought that this right was original found in a provision of the Magna Carta, one of the most important legal documents in history.

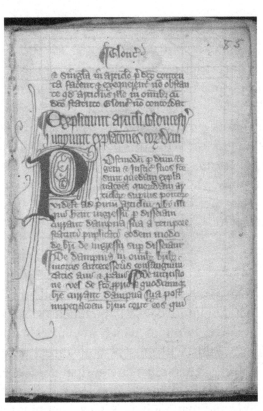

The Magna Carta – Great Charter with English Statutes

The **Sixth Amendment** to the US Constitution States:

"In all criminal prosecutions, the accused shall enjoy the right to a speedy and public trial, by an impartial jury of the State and district wherein the crime shall have been committed, which district shall have been previously ascertained by law, and to be informed of the nature and cause of the accusation; to be confronted with the witnesses against him; to have compulsory process for obtaining witnesses in his favor, and to have the Assistance of Counsel for his defense."

The Magna Carta

This important legal document was written in 1215. It was an agreement between King John I and the barons who were challenging his rule. It required King John of England to provide certain rights, respect certain legal procedures, and accept that he was subject to the law.

The Magna Carta forms the basis of US Democracy and international human rights laws, such as the UN's Universal Declaration of Human Rights.

The US judicial system is based on the concept of common law, which makes it possible for the state and federal governments to follow a common set of trial procedures.

The steps of a criminal trial

A criminal trial has many steps and procedures, all of which are designed to ensure that the accused receives a fair trial based on the available evidence.

Decision by Judge or Jury.

The defense in a criminal trial (the defense attorney and the accused) have the right to choose whether the case will be tried by a judge or a jury. There are pros and cons to each type of trial, so the defense team will carefully consider the risks and benefits based on the circumstances of each case. In some places, both the prosecution and the defense are able to demand a jury trial.

Jury Selection.

One of the first steps of a jury trial is jury selection. This is a joint effort by both the prosecution and the defense. Both sides of the case are able to question potential jurors in a process called "voir dire", meaning to speak the truth. Both the defense and the prosecution have the option of rejecting jurors either for cause or using peremptory challenges. In federal, and some state, courts the judge carries out this process. The judge uses questions proposed by the attorney, as well as questions she develops on her own. The jury usually consists of 6-12 members of the community who are selected from a jury pool. Alternate jurors are also selected. Alternate jurors hear the case with the other jurors, but do not participate in the deliberations unless another juror is removed.

Evidence

Evidence may be included or excluded in the trial. Both the defense and prosecution have a chance to request that certain evidence is included or excluded. This is done using motion "in limine." The judge determines which evidence is admitted and which is not. The prosecution and defense teams will present both direct and circumstantial evidence. Direct evidence speaks for itself. This includes physical evidence, such as a weapon or an eyewitness account. Circumstantial evidence is implied and cannot be directly proven. Both types of evidence are valuable and may include witness testimony or physical exhibits. The type of evidence admitted, as well as the presentation of evidence, is governed by formal rules.

Opening statements

The opening statements are the first chance the attorneys, both defense and prosecution, have to state the outlines of the case to the judge or jury. The prosecution presents the opening statement first, followed by the defense. The prosecution in a case carries the burden of proof, therefore presents first. The prosecution must prove the case beyond a reasonable doubt.

In limine

Latin for "at the threshold." This is a motion that is made before the start of the trial. The motion may request the inclusion or exclusion of evidence from the trial. The judge rules on the motions before the beginning of the trial, determining which evidence the jury will see during the trial.

Occasionally, the defense will request to make their opening statement until the beginning of the defense case. This allows the defense to keep its strategy from the prosecution until after the prosecution has presented its case. Either side may choose not to present an opening argument.

Prosecution Case-in-chief

The case-in-chief consists of the prosecutor presenting its main case through direct examination of prosecution witnesses. The defense may object to individual questions or lines of questioning, which are then sustained or overruled by the judge. If the objection is sustained, the prosecutor has the opportunity to rephrase the question. The only time a prosecutor is allowed to ask leading questions during direct examination is if the witness is deemed hostile, meaning the witness is likely to be prejudiced because of the witness' relationship with the defendant.

Cross-Examination

Cross-examination allows the defense to ask questions of the prosecution witness. The defense attorney may cross-examine the prosecution witness only on topics raised during the prosecution's direct examination. Cross-examination is often used to discredit (impeach) the witness or expose a weakness in the prosecution case. Leading questions are allowed in cross examination.

Redirect

The prosecution may want to ask the prosecution witness more questions after the defense has completed cross examination. If this is the case, the prosecutor requests permission to re-examine the prosecution witness. This may be done to allow the witness to more fully answer a question or to repair damage done by the defense attorney.

Prosecution Rests.

When the prosecution finishes presenting its case, it rests. This means that the prosecution has presented all the evidence it is going to present in the case.

Motion to Dismiss.

Occasionally, the defense may feel that the prosecution did not prove its case enough to support a guilty verdict. When this is the case, the defense will make a motion to dismiss all charges against the defendant. If the motion is granted by the judge, the case is over and the defense does not have to present its case to the jury. This is an optional step in the process.

Denial of Motion to Dismiss

Almost all motions to dismiss are denied by the judge.

Defense Case-in-chief

Just as in the prosecution case-in-chief, the defense presents its case by directly examining the defense witnesses. The defense attorney may or may not choose to put the defendant on the stand to offer evidence.

Cross-examination

In the defense case-in-chief, the prosecution has the opportunity to examine defense witnesses. This is an opportunity to discredit the witnesses or find weaknesses in the defense case that might raise reasonable doubt in the minds of the judge or jury.

Redirect

As with the prosecution case-in-chief, the defense attorney has an opportunity to try to repair damage the prosecutor may have caused to the defense case.

Defense Rests

Once the defense attorney has presented the defense case-in-chief to the judge or jury, the defense will rest its case.

Prosecution Rebuttal

The prosecution has the opportunity to present evidence to refute the defense case. This may be in the form of reminding the jury about key aspects of the prosecution case-in-chief.

Settling on Jury Instructions

Jury instructions are developed by the judge, prosecutor and defense attorney working together. Jury instructions are critical in providing the basis for the jury's deliberations. The instructions are designed to make sure that the jury considers all the evidence presented in the case and understands what it means to be "guilty beyond a reasonable doubt." The attorneys request that the judge include certain instructions, but the judge makes the final decision.

Prosecution Closing Argument

The closing argument is an opportunity for the prosecution to summarize the evidence from the prosecution perspective, remind the jury of weaknesses in the defense case, and try to convince the jury to render a guilty verdict.

Defense Closing Argument

The defense closing argument allows the defense attorney a chance to summarize the defense case, point out any weaknesses in the prosecution case, and encourage the jury to render a not guilty verdict or a guilty verdict on a lesser charge.

Prosecution Rebuttal

The prosecution may choose to rebut the defense closing argument. If the prosecution decides to rebut the defense closing argument, it is yet another opportunity to argue that there is enough evidence to support a guilty verdict.

Jury Instructions

At this point, the defense and prosecution have made their best efforts to present a compelling case to the judge or jury. The judge instructs the jury about the appropriate laws to apply to the case and how to carry out its duties. The jury's job is to decide if the defendant is guilty based on the evidence presented. The jury instructions are called the judge's **charge** to the jury.

Post-trial Motions

The jury may find the defendant guilty or not guilty. If the jury finds the defendant guilty, the defense attorney is likely to make post-trial motions. The motions request the judge to overrule the jury's finding and either grant the defendant a new trial or acquit the defendant.

Denial of Post-Trial Motions

As with the motion to dismiss, judges almost always deny post-trial motions from the defense.

Sentencing

If the jury finds the defendant guilty, the judge has the responsibility of sentencing the defendant. This may happen as soon as the verdict is rendered. It may also be delayed to give the judge time to consider the appropriate sentence.

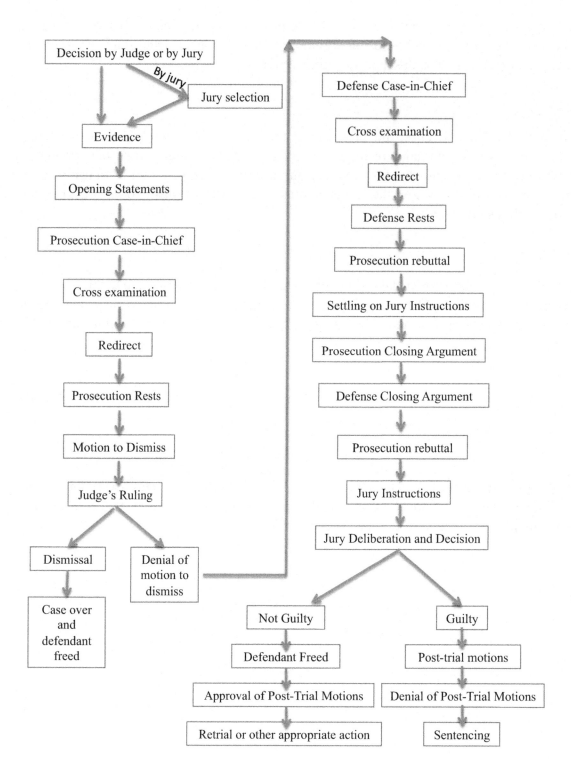

A flowchart of the US trial process.

Summary

The sixth amendment to the US Constitution guarantees the accused the right to a speedy and public trial. This roots of this concept, also called common law, go back to the Magna Carta, which was signed by King John I in the year 1215. The Magna Carta assured that King John I would follow certain legal procedures, respect certain rights, and accept that he was subject to the rule of law like everyone else. Over time, the concepts put forward in the Magna Carta led to Sixth Amendment to the US Constitution and the court system we have in the US. The American court system is designed to ensure that every defendant receives a speedy and public trial by a jury of his peers. The court system may seem ponderous to those of us outside the system, but it works to ensure that the Sixth Amendment is upheld and everyone is able to have a fair and public trial.

. . . .

Concept Reinforcement

1. State briefly what the 6th Amendment to the US Constitution ensures.

2. Describe the impact of the Magna Carta on our modern judicial system.

3. Briefly explain the overall process of a criminal trial.

Chapter 14 – Expert Witnesses

Chapter Objective

- Describe the importance of expert witnesses and how they can influence the outcome of the trial

What is an expert witness?

An expert witness is someone who has more knowledge about a topic than an average person. This expertise allows him to give testimony on an issue that. An expert witness must have the credentials and experience to prove their expert status.

Some of the factors considered when qualifying an expert witness are:

- The number of years they have practiced in their respective field

- Work experience related to the case

- Published works

- Certifications

- Licensing

- Training

- Education

- Awards

- Peer recognition

For example, an expert witness testifying about the mental state of a defendant at the time of the crime must be able to prove her expertise. The court will review and question her education and work experience, publications, certifications and licenses, awards, peer recognition and other measures of her expertise. An expert witness who specializes in criminal behavior and mental health will be more credible than someone who specializes in child psychology.

The *Frye Standard*

The court can accept expert testimony that meets the following tests:

1. The evidence is based on well-recognized scientific principle and discovery.

2. The scientific principle is sufficiently established.

3. The scientific principle has gained general acceptance in the scientific community.

An expert witness is a specialist – someone who is educated in a certain area.
He testifies with respect to his specialty area only.

Expert witnesses may act as consultants to a case and may give testimony at trial. The materials expert witnesses use when developing their opinions are subject to discovery once the expert is listed as a witness for trial. Expert testimony is subject to cross examination, where the opposing counsel may ask questions designed to find weaknesses in the credentials of the expert witness, lack of confidence in his opinions, lack of preparation, or unreliability of the expert's sources, tests, and methods.

The testimony of expert witness will have a strong influence on the outcome of the trial. Expert testimony often carries more weight with the judge and the jury. The opposition will work hard to impeach the credibility of expert witnesses in order to make the testimony less effective. The adversarial nature of our court system makes it very important for expert witnesses to be able to defend their opinions with strong, scientifically accepted documentation of how they developed their opinions. The same applies to their credentials.

Expert witnesses are the only type of witnesses who are allowed to elaborate on the answers they give to questions. Remember that most witnesses are usually allowed to answer only yes or no to the questions posed to them by the attorneys. Expert witnesses, on the other hand, are expected to provide comprehensive, understandable explanations of complex scientific concepts. The explanations provided by the expert witnesses help the jurors to understand the evidence and use the information to determine innocence or guilt.

Standards of Acceptance for Testimony

Standards of acceptance for expert testimony have developed over many years. The first key case is Frye V. United States, which was tried in 1923. This case tested whether polygraph exam results (lie detector test) were admissible as evidence in that particular case. The case resulted in the development of the Frye Standard for presenting scientific evidence to the court. An important aspect of the Frye Standard is that it allows new scientific tests to be used to support expert testimony, but only after the procedures have been thoroughly tested and accepted by the scientific community.

Frye remained the standard of acceptance for expert testimony for many years. It is still followed in many jurisdictions. The practice of law leads to changes in accepted practice and standards. In the case of the Frye Standard, it was recently replaced by Rule 702 of the Federal Rules of Evidence. Rule 702 is the result of Daubert v Merrell Dow Pharmaceutical, Inc. Rule 702 states that judges may use their discretion to admit expert testimony to understand the evidence and to determine a fact in issue. This allows judges the judge more discretion in the expert testimony allowed during a trial. Rule 702 was further supported by the United States Supreme court when it determined that the "general acceptance" clause of Frye is not absolute. This means that judges have the discretion to allow expert witnesses to testify based on scientific findings and techniques that may not have become generally accepted at the time of the trial. This is very important because technology changes very quickly. If the technology or theory is generally reliable and accepted, it may be allowed as expert testimony.

The Supreme Court of the United States

The Supreme Court guidelines provide further guidance on how to determine if a new scientific technique or theory is acceptable to the court. These guidelines state that the new technique or theory must:

- Be subject to testing and to peer review.

- Be standardized with recognized maintenance of such standards.

- Have a known and accepted error rate.

- Attain widespread acceptance.

In practice, this means that any new scientific technique or theory must be clearly stated, tested, reviewed, accepted and continually monitored for accuracy.

The judge and lawyers work out which scientific evidence and testimony will be acceptable before the trial even starts. The judge will allow the evidence that passes the Frye or Daubert standards into testimony. Any evidence that does not pass these standards will not be admitted.

Forensic Experts as Expert Witnesses

Forensic investigators, lab technicians, and the Medical Examiner are often called upon to provide expert testimony in a trial. The ME is responsible for providing clear, unbiased and truthful evidence based on the forensic techniques performed to analyze the evidence. The ME often has to educate the judge and jury in addition to providing expert testimony related to the evidence of the case. This role of educator makes it very important for the ME and the staff o the medical examiner's office to be able to translate complex scientific information into words that accurately describe a concept while making it possible for a lay person to understand the concept.

The images below show expert review of a fire scene. A fire fighter died at this fire. This review was performed by Vincent Dunn, Deputy Chief (Ret.), FDNY. Notice how the photo and the graphic are both clearly labeled to show the locations of people and objects.

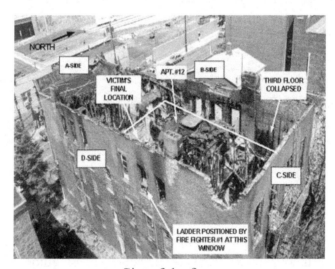

Site of the fire.

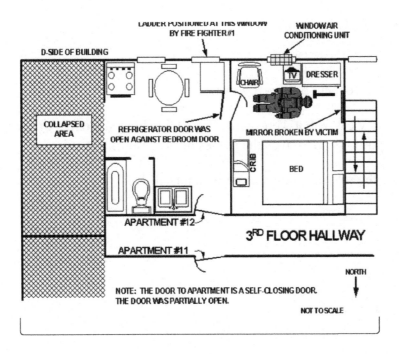

Within the image:

D-SIDE OF BUILDING

LADDER POSITIONED AT THIS WINDOW
BY FIRE FIGHTER #1

WINDOW AIR
CONDITIONING UNIT

TV DRESSER

CHAIR

COLLAPSED
AREA

REFRIGERATOR DOOR WAS
OPEN AGAINST BEDROOM DOOR

MIRROR BROKEN BY VICTIM

CRIB

BED

APARTMENT #12

3RD FLOOR HALLWAY

APARTMENT #11

NORTH

NOTE: THE DOOR TO APARTMENT IS A SELF-CLOSING DOOR.
THE DOOR WAS PARTIALLY OPEN.

NOT TO SCALE

Image courtesy of NIOSH

Summary

Expert testimony is critical to the successful conduct of a trial. Expert witnesses testify in court to provide technical testimony related to specific aspects of the case. The prosecution and defense are both allowed to use expert witnesses, which may result in conflicting testimony from expert witnesses. Expert testimony is not always considered reliable. Questions about the reliability of expert testimony are often tested in court. Two key rulings have shaped the use of expert testimony in court. The first (Frye v United States) resulted in the Frye Standard, which set standards of acceptability for expert testimony. The Frye Standard was revisited during Daubert v Merrell-Dow Pharmaceuticals, Inc. The Daubert case resulted in Rule 702 of the Federal Rules of Evidence. Rule 702 provides the judge greater leeway in choosing which expert witnesses to allow in the court. These two standards are the most commonly used standards for expert witnesses. Forensic experts are often called to provide expert testimony. These expert witnesses must be able to prove their scientific credentials and provide scientific proof to support their findings and opinions. The Medical Examiner often plays a dual role of educator and expert witness. This is an important role. The technical evidence provided in cases is often very complex and difficult to understand. An effective expert witness will be able to explain this complex scientific information in terms that a lay audience is able to understand.

Concept Reinforcement

1. Explain the concept of expert witness.

2. List two key cases that were critical in establishing standards of acceptance for expert testimony, as well as the names of the resulting standards.

3. Describe the role of forensic experts in a trial.

Chapter 15 – The Impact of the Media

Chapter Objectives

- Explain the impact of media on criminal investigations and trials

What is the media?

We have all seen media coverage of high profile criminal investigations. What do we really mean when we talk about "the media"? There are many different types of media, especially now that the Internet is used so widely for spreading information and theories about crimes. Mainstream media include newspapers, radio and television news programs, and news magazines. Internet-based news is becoming more mainstream. It is important to be careful about the Internet resource you use. Some are quite reliable. Others are not subject to any journalistic review or standards. Reliable sources include libraries, professional societies, government agencies, reputable non-profit organizations, universities and other respected groups. Unreliable internet resources include those that can be edited by anyone without outside review. Blogs and other social forums are likely to contain opinions, which are not necessarily fact. It is also important to consider the agenda of the group or person putting information on the web. If someone is pushing a particular agenda, it is possible that the information presented will be biased in some way, so it is important to be aware of the overall motivation of the group.

How does media attention affect criminal investigations?

Crime scenes must be protected and thoroughly investigated in order to identify, collect, document, and transport evidence from the scene of the crime to the crime lab. The police have the job of protecting the crime scene from anyone who wants to see the crime scene before the evidence is collected. They need to prevent family and friends, media, and non-essential law enforcement personnel from entering the crime scene. This prevents damage to crucial evidence, as well as contamination (addition of new evidence to the crime scene). Protection of the crime scene also prevents the release of information about the crime that the police may want to keep from the public while the crime is under investigation. There may be an unusual aspect of the crime that will help the police identify the perpetrator or provide a link to other crimes.

The police need to protect certain evidence from disclosure, particularly if the crime has unusual characteristics, such as use of an unusual weapon, which will help identify the perpetrator. They may also want to prevent disclosure of evidence that might connect serial crimes, and potentially cause public concern or panic. It is important for the police to be able to hold back certain critical pieces of evidence while they are investigating.

Like the crime scene, the crime lab must be secure. Lab personnel must be free of undue influence from aggressive members of the media who want exclusive interviews or access to evidence that has been kept from the public to help the police investigation. The lab is responsible for maintaining the chain of custody of the evidence. It is very important that evidence is not leaked to the media, stolen or damaged in order to maintain the integrity of the evidence, as well as the chain of custody of the evidence. If the evidence is compromised, it may not be admissible in court or be less useful for solving the crime and prosecuting the accused.

How does media attention affect the conduct of the trial?

The media influence all aspects of a trial. High profile cases often make it difficult or impossible for an unbiased jury to be selected in the area the crime occurred. In cases like this, the trial may have to be moved to another jurisdiction, at great expense to the public court system, in order to ensure a fair trial to the accused. In some cases, the jury may be sequestered to prevent the jurors from talking to anyone, particularly the media, about the details of the case. This adds to the cost of the trial and the stress to the jurors because they live in a hotel, are under guard 24 hours a day, and are unable to communicate with anyone outside the jury and the court. They may not even be able to talk with their families during the trial.

Courtroom sketch of Mounir el Motassadeq, on trial 22 October 2002,
in Hamburg, Germany, for allegedly aiding the Hamburg terrorist cell involved
in the September 11 attacks. Image courtesy of US State Department.

Once the trial begins, the media report on the courtroom events. In most cases, this is not a problem. However, in cases that are interesting to the public (celebrities, particularly brutal crime etc), the media coverage can make it difficult to conduct the trial properly. Think about some of the high profile cases you may have seen or heard about. Do you think it would be possible to maintain an objective jury and protect the rights of the defendant and witnesses with extensive and aggressive media coverage?

Think about the OJ Simpson Trial. There were 133 days of televised courtroom testimony during the 1995 trial. In fact, of the people watching television the day the verdict was announced, 91% were watching the trial. The courtroom proceedings were dissected by various pundits (people who talk as experts about issues on television), gossiped about in homes and workplaces, and dominated the news. The media coverage had a strong influence on public opinion about the trial. It also caused problems during the trial because of the distraction presented by the intensity of the media interest in the daily proceedings. In fact, some of the evidence the prosecution was planning to present was not actually used at trial. Two pieces of evidence are the knife used in the murders and the testimony of a witness who saw a white Ford Bronco leaving the scene in a hurry. In both cases, the testimony was excluded because the people sold their stories to media outlets before the trial.

Witness and Jury Tampering

Another concern in high profile cases is the safety and security of the accused, witnesses, jury, judge and attorneys. Witnesses may be in protective custody because of threats to their health; concerns about witness tampering, or other concerns for their safety. Jurors may also be in protective custody to prevent jury tampering and protect them from potential threats. **Jury tampering** occurs when someone, usually from the defense, attempts to influence the deliberations of the jury by paying or threatening a juror to get a specific outcome in favor of the defendant. **Witness tampering** is the same. Sometimes a witness can be influenced to change testimony, by either a threat or a payoff.

The jury is a key part of the judicial system. The jury helps ensure
that the accused is judged by a jury of his or her peers.
Image Courtesy of US District Court for the District of Columbia.

In certain sensitive or high profile cases, the judge may even **close the courtroom**. This is a rare decision that must be approved through a legal process before it is implemented. Remember that the Sixth Amendment to the US Constitution guarantees a defendant a speedy and public trial. There are certain compelling reasons that allow the public involvement to be limited.

Federal Officers on Guard Duty
Image courtesy of the US Department of the Interior.

The process used to close courtroom proceedings requires the party seeking closure (defense or prosecution) to prove an **overriding interest** that the trial is likely to be prejudiced if kept open. The courtroom may be closed for the entire trial or only for specific proceedings. It is important to understand that the decision to close courtroom proceedings must be limited to only those parts of the trial that warrant such protections. Closure is often requested to protect the identity of police officers, usually undercover officers. Closure may also be requested if there are concerns that evidence that could be subject to suppression is going to be presented and has the potential to prejudice the defendant's later right to a fair trial.

If a closure occurs, only those who are required to be in the courtroom will be allowed to enter. The general public and the media are not allowed in the courtroom during the closed portion of the trial

Cameras in the courtroom.

In general, cameras are not allowed in the courtroom. Reporters and sketch artists are allowed to watch trials. Reporters may take notes and the sketch artist draw various courtroom scenes. The policy on cameras in the courtroom varies by jurisdiction. The federal courts and the District of Columbia do not allow televised coverage of court proceedings. Some state courts do allow televised coverage of courtroom proceedings under certain conditions. In some states, the trial judge has to agree to the cameras. In other states, cameras are allowed in the courtroom only if all trial participants agree to the cameras. Still other states allow television coverage of only appellate proceedings.

The 1965 Supreme Court case, Estes v. Texas, the defendant (Estes) claimed that the television coverage of the trial denied him a fair trial. The Supreme Court agreed with him and determined that live television coverage was distracting to jurors, judges, and defendants and was likely to impair witness testimony.

This ruling was changed in 1981, when the Supreme Court agreed in a unanimous vote that the State of Florida could allow radio, television and still photographic coverage of a criminal trial, regardless of whether the defendant agreed. The Supreme Court Justices concluded that the majority of those who ruled in Estes v. Texas did not rule that broadcast coverage or photography of a trial was a denial of due process. This ruling (Chandler) resulted in most states establishing laws allowing cameras in some state courts.

The reasons for excluding cameras from courtrooms remain the same as they were in 1965 when Estes was argued. In general, the courts agree that live television coverage:

- Distracts trial participants

- Unfairly affects the outcome of trials

- Diminishes the dignity of the courts.

- The Sunshine Laws

As you may expect, journalists have pushed back against having limited access to trials and the courts. Many lawsuits have been filed and cases argued regarding public access to governmental records. Governmental records include the prosecution files on cases they have argued or are actively being prosecuted. The result of these lawsuits is a range of laws known as sunshine laws, open records laws, or public record laws. Collectively, they are known as **Freedom of Information Act (FOIA)** laws. Each state has unique laws about how individuals can gain access to government information.

Sunshine laws have led to a change in the relationship between the media and the police and other crime investigators. Sunshine laws allow reporters to request information about police investigations through the Freedom of Information Act by making a FOIA request for information. When this occurs, the agency receiving the request has the burden of proof if they want to withhold any information.

In general, police are there to serve the public and want to be both responsible and responsive to the public. However, as we discussed earlier in this sections, releasing information about an ongoing criminal investigation can compromise the ability of the police to solve the crime. It can also have a negative impact on the prosecution of the case. There have been cases where the media criticized the police for not releasing information, which then resulted in extensive public criticism. Sometimes the criticism is warranted, but usually it is not warranted. The police need to have some discretion in pursuing their investigations without releasing every bit of information they have about the case. There may be concerns about copycat crimes or other public reactions that will compromise the investigation.

An example of a publicly accessible trial occurred with U.S. v. Zacaria Moussaoui, which started in 2002 and ended with a conviction and life sentence without the chance of parole in 2006. This case was tried in the Eastern District of Virginia, which continues to update its web pages with information about the trial.

Moussaui was accused of participating in the 9/11 attacks in 2001. Public Law 107-206 permitted victims of crimes associated with the terrorist attacks of 9/11 to watch the trial proceedings. It further ordered the trial court to set up closed circuit television (CCTV) to televise the proceedings to locations set up for the victims of the attacks.

The U.S. District Court for the Eastern District of Virginia posted copies to its website of approximately 1,200 exhibits admitted into evidence during the trial in U.S. v. Zacarias Moussaoui—providing public access to nearly every exhibit viewed by the jury. As shown in the illustration by artist William Hennessy, exhibits were displayed throughout the courtroom on TV monitors.
Image courtesy of uscourts.gov.

One very interesting aspect of this case is that all of the pieces of evidence (approximately 1,200) admitted during the trial are available to anyone worldwide who has access to the Internet. Remember that government records, including court records are subject to FOIA. The court decided that the high profile nature of the case warranted posting images of the evidence on a web site, which would provide efficient access, both from the perspective of the person looking for information and for the clerk's office that has to provide the information.

Summary

The media have the potential to influence a trial both positively and negatively. If the media work with police during the investigation of a crime, it can help the police gather critical evidence, which will then help them solve the crime. On the negative side, excess publicity or leaking of critical evidence can have a negative impact on both the investigation and the trial. The Sunshine Laws provide members of the public access to governmental records if requests are made following the protocol required by FOIA. The sunshine laws can make it difficult for investigators to hold back evidence in a case. The police often keep key evidence from the public because it will help them solve the crime. Once the crime is solve and trial complete, the evidence may be released in response to a FOIA request. The challenge for the police is proving that the requested information or evidence should not be subject to FOIA. The burden of proof falls on the government, not the requestor.

. . . .

Concept Reinforcement

1. Describe how the media can affect the collection of evidence from a crime scene.

2. Explain why cameras are not generally allowed in courtrooms.

3. State the purpose of the sunshine laws.

Chapter 16 – Crime Scene Investigation

Chapter Objective

- Describe the crime scene investigation unit and its role in forensic investigations

The Crime Scene Investigation Unit

Crime scene investigation is very different from TV

You have probably watched the crime scene investigation (CSI) units in action as they are shown on television dramas such as *CSI Miami*. However, these shows are not very accurate when it comes to real life crime scene investigation.

In reality, a CSI unit collects and preserves the evidence found at a crime scene. Evidence collection is meticulous work that requires intense focus and attention to detail. Once the evidence is collected, the CSI unit transports it to the crime lab to be processed and to maintain the chain of custody required to use the evidence in a criminal trial.

The members of a CSI unit collect all types of evidence, including fingerprints, fibers (clothing, furniture fabric, carpet, etc.), hair, blood, bullet casings, and many other items that might help the police solve the crime at hand. They may also sketch the scene or take photographs to document the scene.

CSI unit members do NOT interrogate suspects, carry guns (unless they have a private permit), or make arrests like they do on TV. Their main role is the collection and preservation of evidence at the scene of a crime.

A criminalist collecting evidence

A crime scene investigator (CSI) may also be called a **crime scene analyst (CSA)** or **crime scene technician** depending on what jurisdiction they work within. This is a broad job title that includes many different specialties. Many times CSIs are trained civilians that are hired by the police department to collect and process evidence at the crime scene. Others are members of the police department that have been trained in crime scene investigation. Once evidence is collected it is sent to the crime lab for further analysis by specialized laboratory personnel called **criminalists**. Some examples of specialized labs include: Firearms/Ballistics, Arson Investigation, Questioned Documents, Fingerprint Analysis, DNA Analysis, Trace Evidence, and many others.

Crime scene investigators have many different tools they use to help them collect and preserve evidence on the job. The following table lists some of the important items that a criminalist may use at a typical crime scene. There are many other items that a criminalist may need to carry depending on the type of crime and evidence that needs to be collected.

Crime Scene Investigator Tool	Purpose
Crime Scene Tape	Mark and secure the crime scene
Camera, evidence ruler	Photograph the scene and evidence
Sketchpad and pens	Sketch scene
Personal Protective Gear	Disposable clothing such as masks and gloves to protect the crime scene investigators and avoid contamination of evidence
Flashlight	Provide light in dark or small spaces
UV light source	Search for specific types of evidence, such as blood or other body fluids that may not be visible to the naked eye
Magnifying glass	Help locate trace evidence

Paper and plastic evidence bags, glass tubes, tweezers	Collect and transport evidence
Fingerprint supplies: Fingerprint powder, fiberglass brushes, clear tape, print cards, ink pad	Find and collect fingerprints
Casting supply kit	Making casts of foot prints, tire tracks, or other impressions at the crime scene.
Serology kit: needles, syringes, etc.	Collection of blood and other body fluids from victim or persons at scene
Hazardous materials kit	Handing and collecting hazardous materials

A criminalist dusting a casing for fingerprints

Summary

The crime scene investigation unit is responsible for the collection and preservation of evidence at a crime scene. A crime scene investigator, also called a crime scene analyst or crime scene technician, is trained to properly collect and preserve evidence at a scene to maintain the chain of custody. This is important in order for evidence to be submitted for usage at a criminal trial. Once evidence is collected it is sent to the crime lab for analysis. These analyses are done within specialized departments of the crime lab by criminalists. A crime scene investigator must be highly trained and have great attention to detail in order to successfully perform their job.

. . . .

Concept Reinforcement

1. Describe the main role of a crime scene investigator.

2. List several items that a typical crime scene investigator would carry in their kit to a crime scene.

3. Why is it important to maintain the chain of custody when collecting evidence?

Chapter 17 – Forensic Pathology

Chapter Objective

- Explain forensic pathology and its applications

What is forensic pathology?

Pathology is the study of the origin, nature, and course of disease. **Forensic pathology** is a subspecialty of pathology that looks at how and why people die. A **forensic pathologist** is a medical doctor that attends a specialized residency program in forensic pathology. There are a limited number of board certified forensic pathologists in the United States. During their training, a forensic pathologist will perform autopsies, attend death scenes, and study many disciplines of forensics including ballistics, serology, toxicology, odontology, radiology, and anthropology. The most important function performed by a forensic pathologist is deciding how and why a person died. They may be called upon to defend these diagnoses in a court of law. Forensic pathologists work in either a medical examiner's office or a coroner's office depending on the state and jurisdiction they are working within. Although run differently from state to state, these offices are responsible for investigating sudden, traumatic, and/or suspicious deaths.

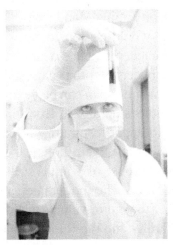

A forensic pathologist is an integral part of a death investigation

What exactly does a forensic pathologist do?

The medical examiner (ME) or coroner is the central figure in a death investigation. They oversee the gathering of information at a scene and during the autopsy procedure if one is conducted. The ME or coroner may or may not be the person conducting the autopsy (depending on if they are the forensic pathologist as well), however this information is combined with the scene investigation data to make a conclusion about a particular death. It is the forensic pathologist's responsibility to rule on the cause and manner of death involved. Once the cause and manner of death are determined by the forensic pathologist, they will sign the death certificate to verify their findings. They may be called upon at a later date to testify as an expert witness during a criminal or civil trial.

The coroner or medical examiner is the central figure of a death investigation

What is the difference between the manner and cause of death?

A forensic pathologist must determine the manner and cause of death involved in a case by conducting a thorough autopsy and analysis of information gathered at the scene. The **cause of death** is the actual injury or disease which ultimately led to the death of an individual. Cause of death can be considered either proximate or immediate. **Proximate cause of death** is the underlying or original condition that led to the **immediate cause of death**. For instance, breast cancer would be considered a proximate cause of death, while the pneumonia that led to a breast cancer patient's death would be considered the immediate cause of death. The time period between the proximate and immediate cause of death can be minutes, hours, weeks, or years. The time span can be years for example if a person is injured in an automobile accident and becomes paralyzed from the neck down (quadriplegic). This patient then becomes susceptible to upper respiratory infections and eventually many years later dies of severe respiratory infection. Even though the person did not die immediately following the accident, the proximate cause of death is still the original injury from the motor vehicle crash which left him paralyzed. The immediate cause of death would be the severe respiratory infection. In this case, if the motor vehicle accident was caused by a drunk driver, a civil case may be filed by the family and the forensic pathologist may be called to testify on their behalf.

A proximate cause of death such as a motor vehicle accident may occur many years before the actual death occurs.

There is also a further distinction made concerning the immediate cause of death called the **mechanism of death**. This is the actual biochemical or physiological abnormality that resulted in the death. For instance, the mechanism of death behind pneumonia many times is septicemia (which means infection). Other mechanisms of death include ventricular fibrillation, shock, or cardiorespiratory arrest. These mechanisms cannot be listed as the cause of death on a death certificate. The proximate cause of death is what is listed as the primary cause of death, with the immediate causes sometimes listed as secondary. For example, a particular case may list the cause of death as a gunshot wound to the head secondary to major blood loss.

The **manner of death** is different from the cause of death. The manner of death is the circumstances surrounding a death and is typically placed in one of the following categories:

- Homicide

- Suicide

- Accident

- Natural

- Undetermined

The individual discussed above that died due to the paralysis from the motor vehicle crash would have a manner of death listed as accidental. If the driver of the other vehicle was under the influence, the manner of death could be classified as homicide. Look at the following table which gives some examples that differentiate between the different classifications of cause and manner of death.

Proximate Cause	Intermediate Cause	Mechanism	Manner
Traumatic injuries from an MVA (motor vehicle accident)	cerebral hemorrhage	Ventricular fibrillation	Accident
Severe burns (from house fire)	hemorrhagic shock	cardiorespiratory arrest	Homicide
Coronary Artery Disease	cardiorespiratory arrest due to blockage	cardiorespiratory arrest	Natural

Examples of classifications of death

Summary

A forensic pathologist is a specialized pathologist that looks at how and why people die. They are responsible for ruling on the cause and manner of death for an individual. They do this by completing a thorough autopsy and analysis of the information gathered at the scene. The cause of death is the actual injury or disease that resulted in the death of an individual. It can be divided into a proximate and immediate cause of death. The manner of death includes the circumstances surrounding the death and can be ruled as homicide, suicide, accident, natural, or undetermined.

Concept Reinforcement

1. What responsibilities does a forensic pathologist have?

2. What is the difference between proximate and immediate cause of death?

3. What are the classifications for manner of death?

Chapter 18 – Forensic Autopsy

Chapter Objective

- Describe a forensic autopsy

What is a forensic autopsy?

The word **autopsy** is taken from an ancient Greek word literally meaning "to view for oneself". An autopsy is done to determine the cause of death and describe pathological conditions of the body. Autopsies can be conducted in a general medical setting for research purposes or in a forensic setting to investigate sudden, traumatic or suspicious deaths. A forensic pathologist conducts **forensic autopsies** to determine the cause and manner of death. This involves a thorough external and internal examination.

A typical autopsy room where forensic pathologists work

External Examination

The first task of the forensic pathologist during an autopsy is to conduct a detailed external examination. This information is recorded as part of a documented report. The first things that are recorded include clothing and jewelry worn, racial status, scars or tattoos present, height of the body from heel to head, weight, physical description (hair color, eye color, etc.) The external exam also records the following information:

Preservation

The condition of the body is recorded according to the level of decomposition. A body that has not started the decomposition process it is recorded as good. Once decomposition begins, the condition can be recorded as early decomposition, putrid, or skeletonised. The rate of decomposition can be affected by environmental conditions. Higher temperatures accelerate the process.

Temperature

The temperature of the body is typically taken at the death scene by the deputy coroner or medical examiner by inserting a temperature probe through the skin into the liver. This may help to estimate the time of death. During the autopsy, the pathologist notes the apparent body temperature as warm, cool, cold, or frozen.

Rigor Mortis

Rigor mortis is the stiffening of the muscles following death. Immediately after death occurs, the muscles are flaccid (loose). Within a few hours after death, the muscles and joints begin to stiffen starting with the jaw through a process known as rigor mortis. This process occurs over approximately 24 hours. Full rigor of all muscles and joints of the body occurs approximately 12 to 16 hours into the process. Over the remaining half of the 24 hour period, rigor begins to leave the body in the same order until it becomes flaccid and flexible again. The rigor mortis process can be accelerated or slowed down due to body and environmental temperature. Higher temperatures speed up the process of rigor mortis, while cold temperatures slow the process down. The level of rigor is noted on the external exam as absent, moderate, full, or passed. The level of rigor can help give an estimate of the time of death and indicate if a body has been moved after death occurred.

Livor Mortis

Livor mortis (also known as lividity) is the discoloration of portions of the body after death due to the settling of blood in the tissues. This occurs after death because the heart stops pumping the blood and settles in the tissues. The blood settles in the tissues according to gravity and causes a reddish or purple discoloration of the skin of dependent areas. For instance, if a person dies while lying on their back, livor mortis will occur along the back and rear portion of the extremities. There may be some areas that do not show discoloration because of pressure points of bony surfaces such as the scapulae and buttocks. Livor mortis becomes noticeable within 1 hour after death, but takes approximately 8 to 12 hours to become fixed. Once it is fixed, it will not blanche (turn white) when pressed on externally. The forensic pathologist uses the amount of blanching to rate the level of livor mortis as absent, non-fixed, or fixed in nature. Variations in the color of livor mortis can occur depending upon the cause of death, resulting in pink or purple colorations. For instance, carbon monoxide poisoning will cause bright pink livor mortis coloration. Livor mortis can help determine if a body has been repositioned after death. For example, if livor mortis is noted on the ventral (front) and dorsal (back) aspects of the body, it would indicate that the body was moved after death occurred.

Other observations

Other features that are observed and recorded during the external physical examination include:

- Level of nutrition: adequate, cachetic (extremely thin/malnutritioned), or obese. The presence of any jaundice, edema (swelling), or cyanosis (blue coloration due to low oxygen) is also noted.

- Eyes: The color of the eyes is recorded as well as the presence of any cataracts. The amount of pupil dilation is also noted.

- Hair: Coloration of the hair and the presence of any moustaches and beards are recorded.

- Teeth: The amount of teeth present or absent and the condition of the teeth are noted.

- Medical interventions: EKG patches, tubes, IV sites, catheters, pacemakers, old scar/surgery sites, etc.

- Signs of trauma: Any signs of trauma are recorded and measured for the record. Many times in cases of homicide, trauma is photographed or videotaped a as evidence. These can include any of the following:

- Contusions (brusing)

- Abrasions (minor cut or scrapes)

- Lacerations (break of the skin)

- Punctures (deeper penetration of the skin)

- Incisions

- Amputations

- Fractures

- Gunshot wounds

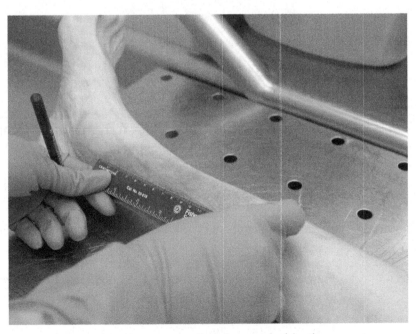

Any trauma is measured and recorded in the report

Internal Examination

Once the external examination is complete, the internal examination begins with a Y-incision down the chest and abdomen from the sternum to the pubic bone. The skin is then reflected and the chest plate removed to access the internal chest and abdominal cavities. The organs are then removed either in a complete block (Rokitansky method) or one at a time (Virchow method). The latter method is most common during a forensic autopsy. Each organ is weighed and dissected by the forensic pathologist to look for any abnormalities. Next, the cranial cavity is opened using a specialized saw and the brain is removed, weighed, and dissected. All the findings are dictated and recorded in the autopsy report. Samples of the internal organs may be preserved for later microscopic testing. All of these findings can help to diagnose a cause of death. Other evidence collected during the autopsy procedure is summarized in the table below.

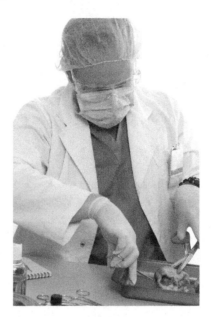

Organs are weighed and dissected by the forensic pathologist

Evidence	Description
Blood	Blood is collected for toxicology testing (drug screening, etc.), blood typing, and DNA comparisons.
Urine	Urine may be used to screen for drugs to determine if a blood analysis is necessary.
Anal, Oral, and/or Vaginal Swabs	In cases of suspected rape, cotton swabs are used to collect any seminal fluid.
Foreign Material	Hair and fiber samples left on the body may be collected in suspicious deaths for later analysis.
Clothing	Clothing is dried and preserved in cases of homicide or suspicious deaths.

Hair	Scalp hair samples from the deceased may be taken in homicide cases. Pubic hair is collected in cases of sexual assault.
Vitreous Humor	The internal fluid of the eye may be drawn and preserved for drug testing and other analysis when urine is not available.
Gastric Contents	Volume and description of the type of food in the stomach is noted. May help identify approximate time of death.

Typical evidence collected during an autopsy

All of the evidence collected during the internal and external examination is used to generate a final autopsy report. The forensic pathologist summarizes their findings and makes a determination of the cause and manner of death.

Summary

A forensic autopsy is conducted to by a forensic pathologist to determine the cause and manner of death. A complete external and internal examination is conducted and the findings are documented in a detailed report. Evidence collected during the autopsy may be used for further analysis to help to diagnose the cause of death.

. . . .

Concept Reinforcement

1. What is the purpose of a forensic autopsy?

2. Define the terms rigor mortis and livor mortis. What can the observation of these variables tell a forensic pathologist?

3. What is the purpose of the internal examination during an autopsy?

Chapter 19 – Fingerprint Analysis

Chapter Objective

- Describe the importance of fingerprint analysis and the techniques used to identify individuals

What is a fingerprint?

Fingerprints consist of the unique friction ridges found on the palm surface of the fingers and thumbs. These friction ridges form a distinct pattern of hills (ridges) and valleys (grooves) and are caused by the shape of the boundary between the **epidermis** (upper layer) and **dermis** (deep layer) of the skin. This boundary area is formed as a result of projections of the dermis into the epidermis, called **dermal papillae**, which anchor the two layers together. The pattern formed by the dermal papillae is unique to each person. The ridge pattern is left as a fingerprint on surfaces when they are touched due to perspiration that is released from the surrounding pores onto the surface of the fingertips. This creates an impression of the fingerprint pattern onto the surface. Fingerprints are a unique identifying characteristic of an individual and no two have ever been found to possess identical characteristics. Fingerprints remain unchanged throughout life and therefore are a reliable means of identification of individuals.

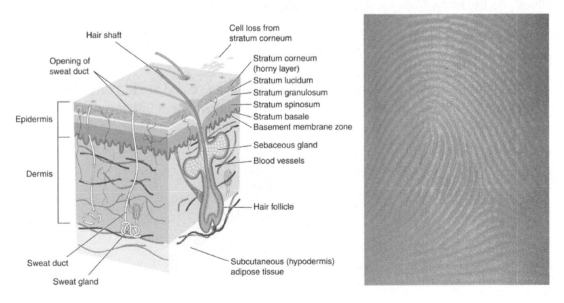

The dermal papillae can be viewed in the above cross section of human skin (left) as the dark purple wavy line between the epidermis and dermis. These create the friction ridges seen in the close up of the fingertip on the right.

The fingerprint details of most interest to a forensic scientist are the ridge characteristics and the general pattern they produce. These are the detailed locations of ridge endings, bifurcations, and enclosures contained within a fingerprint. This also includes one of three general categories of patterns: loops, whorls, and arches. These categories can be further broken down into subcategories such as a radial loop, plain whorl, tented arch, and many more. Fingerprints are classified by using a combination of ridge characteristics and patterns.

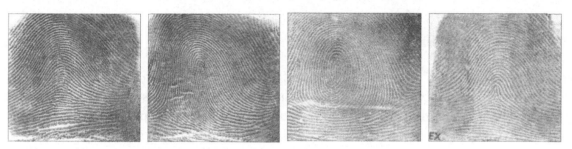

Ridge patterns (left to right): arch, right loop, whorl, and tented arch

How are fingerprints detected?

There are three different types of prints that can be found at a crime scene. These include:

- **Visible prints**: These types of prints are made when the fingers touch a particular surface after they have been in contact with a colored material such as paint, grease, or blood. As the name implies, these prints are visible to the naked eye.

- **Plastic prints**: A plastic print is left when ridge impressions are preserved in a soft surface such as wax or putty materials.

- **Latent prints**: Latent prints are invisible to the naked eye and are left on surfaces due to the transfer of body perspiration and oils on the finger ridges onto a surface.

A visible bloody fingerprint (left) next to a latent print (right)
that has been enhanced with dusting powder.

Finding visible and plastic prints are easiest for an investigator to locate since they are visible to the naked eye. The location of latent prints is harder and may require several different techniques. Prints that are left on hard, nonporous surfaces (glass, tile, painted wood) are typically developed using specialized fingerprint powders. Prints that are found on softer, porous surfaces require treatments of several different chemicals to expose the prints. But, how does the investigator find the print in the first place? The development of ultraviolet imaging systems has helped forensic scientists locate latent prints. When the UV light is shined onto a surface, it reflects light back to the viewer from the fingerprint and is converted into visible light through an image intensifier. This allows the print to be separated from the background. Once a print is discovered, it can be developed using powders or other methods. Look at the table to read about some of the different techniques for visualizing latent prints.

Technique	Description
Fingerprint powder	Fingerprint powder comes in a variety of different colors. They are applied using a camel-hair or fiberglass brush and adhere to perspiration residue on the surface.
Iodine fuming	The material with suspected prints is placed into a chamber with iodine crystals which are heated and adhere to the prints making it visible.
Ninhydrin	Ninhydrin is sprayed from an aerosol can onto the surface. Prints appear within one or two hours of application.
Physical Developer	A chemical mixture of silver-nitrate reagent is applied to a surface to expose prints. This works well on porous surfaces that were once wet.
Super glue fuming	The surface with suspected prints is placed in a chamber and absorbent cotton with super glue applied is heated. The fumes cause the latent prints to appear on the surface after approximately 6 hours in the chamber. There are small hand held wands that allow super glue fuming to be conducted at a crime scene.
Laser light	When latent prints are exposed to laser light they will fluoresce.
High intensity/ alternative light sources	Surfaces are treated with chemicals and then illuminated under an alternative light source (quartz halogen or xenon-arc) which is directed through a fiber-optic cable. Lightweight, portable alternative light sources utilizing LEDs are available for use at a crime scene to search for prints.

Techniques for fingerprint visualization

Crime scene investigator dusting for fingerprints on a door knob.

How are fingerprints preserved?

Once a latent print has been identified, it needs to be preserved permanently for future comparison and possible use as evidence in court. First, a photograph is taken of the print using a specially designed close-up lens. The eye of the lens is placed flush against the print surface to capture its ridge details. Once the photographs are taken, if the object containing the print is small enough it is transported in it's entirely to the lab. If the object is too large, the print must be preserved at the scene. The most popular method of print preservation is the lifting technique. This technique uses adhesive tape to lift a copy of the ridge details of a fingerprint once it has been dusted with powder. The tape is placed over the fingerprint with the sticky side down and is lifted off carrying a copy of the fingerprint. The tape is placed on a card with a background which provides a good contrast for the color in which the print is preserved. ✦

Specialized camera lens are used to create a close up photograph of fingerprints.

How are fingerprints analyzed and compared?

A fingerprint that is preserved through lifting is not always in perfect condition. This can provide challenges to a fingerprint analyst. Advancement of computer technologies has allowed for better analysis and comparison of fingerprints. **Digital imaging** software is utilized to help sharpen an image of a print lifted from a scene. The print is scanned into the computer and the image is digitally enhanced by separating the image from the background. Digital imaging also allows the borders of the ridge edges to be sharpened into better focus. Once the image is enhanced this same program can be used to compare prints. A fingerprint analyst conducts a **point-by-point comparison** of ridge characteristics between two prints. An average of 12 ridge characteristic matches needs to be charted in order to make a positive match between two prints. The advent of **Automated Fingerprint Identification Systems (AFIS)** has made it possible to classify and store fingerprint records for comparison. In 1999, the FBI began full operation of the largest AFIS system in the United States which links the systems of many different local agencies. Unfortunately, it is difficult to link the systems from state to state because of software issues. The AFIS machine scans a digital image of a print into a computer and automatically converts ridge detail data into a file. This database can then be used to look for a match to a set of prints found at a crime scene. Unlike the CSI TV dramas however, the computer cannot make a positive match between two prints. It will compile a list of prints with the closest correlation to the suspect prints. An expert must then look at the prints using a visual analysis to make a positive match. In police precincts nationwide, the old methods of rolling prints from inked fingers onto a card has been replaced with digital-capture machines called livescans. These machines capture an image of the entire surface of the hand preserving the ridge details of the fingertips and palms. These images are then automatically entered in the AFIS system.

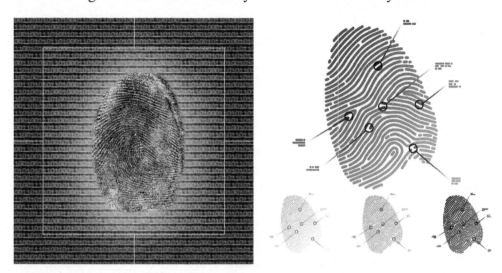

Prints are scanned into the computer and a digital image is created.
Point-by-point comparisons must be confirmed through the visual analysis
of an expert to make a final match.

Concept Extension: Can you erase your own fingerprints?

Perhaps you've seen a movie or a show on TV that shows a criminal that has erased their own fingerprints so they cannot be identified. Can this really be done? In the 1930s a famous bank robber, John Dillinger, attempted to destroy his own prints by pouring a corrosive acid to the skin of his fingertips. Although it did cause scarring, there were still comparable ridge details left that helped police to positively identify him when he was shot at the age of 31 in 1934. Damage to the dermal papillae will not destroy all ridge details and scarring provides a new pattern of characteristics that can then be used in future comparisons.

Summary

Fingerprints are made up of the unique friction ridges found on the palm side of the fingers and thumbs. They are created by the dermal papillae that connect the dermis to the epidermis of the skin. Fingerprints are unique to each individual and remain the same throughout life. Fingerprints are classified according to specific ridge characteristics and patterns. These characteristics can later be used to make a comparison between fingerprints found at a scene and from a suspect. Fingerprints are classified as either visible, plastic, or latent. Latent prints are found through many different methods and are then preserved most commonly through the lifting technique. Once a fingerprint is preserved, it is scanned and digitally enhanced where it can be compared with other prints. The AFIS system is a large database that allows the comparison of digital prints. A positive match between two prints however can only be made through a visual point-by-point comparison done by an expert.

Concept Reinforcement

1. What is a fingerprint?

2. What are the three types of prints that can be found at a scene?

3. What is done to make a positive fingerprint comparison match?

Chapter 20 – Blood Spatter Analysis

Chapter Objective

- Describe the importance of blood spatter analysis and the techniques used to identify individuals

What is blood spatter analysis?

Blood spatter analysis attempts to reconstruct a crime scene using the number, shape, and patterns made with blood evidence from a crime. A criminalist that specializes in blood spatter analysis may be called upon to help with reconstruction of a crime where blood is involved. When a blood spatter expert is called in to work on a case, they must first answer three questions:

1. Is it blood?

2. Is it human in origin?

3. Who does the blood belong to?

Once they answer these questions, they can then conduct an analysis of the pattern of blood splatter found at the scene and provide valuable input into the crime reconstruction process.

The first question a blood spatter analyst must answer is if the substance is in fact human blood.

Is it blood?

Is the substance investigators found at a scene blood or something else? This is the first question that needs to be answered when suspected blood is found at a crime scene. The most common test used to test for the presence of blood in a sample is the **Kastle-Meyer test**. This test uses a chemical known as **phenolphthalein** mixed with hydrogen peroxide to determine if a sample could be blood. When the phenolphthalein, hydrogen peroxide, and the sample are mixed it will turn a deep pink color in the presence of blood. This is due to a reaction with the enzymes found within the **hemoglobin** of blood. This test is called a **presumptive test** since it can positively identify if the substance is NOT blood, but cannot verify that it is indeed blood. It can also be positive for other substances such as horseradish and therefore further testing is needed after a positive Kastle-Meyer test to confirm that the substance is blood.

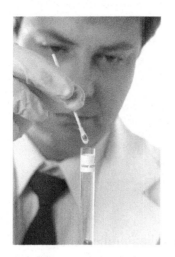

The Kastle-Meyer test is a presumptive test used to indicate the possible presence of blood in a sample.

Another commonly used presumptive test uses **luminol**. A luminol test that is positive causes the substance to **fluoresce** or "glow in the dark". Luminol can be sprayed over large areas to look for the presence of blood. The sprayed objects must be viewed in darkness to look for the glowing effect. It is an extremely sensitive test that can detect blood stains that have been diluted by up to 300,000 times. This is very effective in finding blood at a scene after the perpetrator has attempted to clean it up. Luminol does not interfere with later DNA testing for identification purposes.

Is it human blood?

Once the substance is confirmed as blood, the investigator must be sure that it is human blood. A serologist uses a specialized test known as a **precipitin test** to determine if the blood is indeed human in nature. The human precipitin test exposes the blood sample to a human antiserum. The antibodies in the antiserum react specifically with human antigens and cause a reaction. A positive reaction shows a distinct band within the sample between the antiserum and the blood where the reaction between the two liquids occurred. This is called a precipitin band. Precipitin tests are highly sensitive and can be used on human bloodstains that are ten to fifteen years old. They have even been used to test for blood in mummies found that are over five thousand years old!

Precipitin tests can be used to test for the presence of human blood in samples that are over five thousand years old.

Who does the blood belong to?

Once the investigator knows that the substance is human blood, the next relevant question becomes who does the blood belong to? In the past, blood samples were characterized using the ABO classification system, but today that has been replaced by **DNA profiling**. DNA profiling can provide an exact match between a blood sample and its respective owner. Blood samples from suspected perpetrators of a crime can be collected and tested for a DNA match to blood evidence at a scene. DNA can also be used to identify the victim of a homicide by matching a sample collected from victim's personal effects (razor, toothbrush, etc.) to blood that is found at the crime scene.

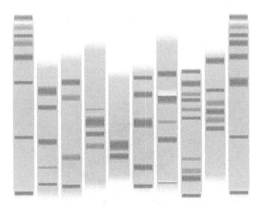

DNA profiling is used to match a blood sample to an individual.

What can blood spatter patterns tell investigators?

Blood spatter analysis at a crime scene is a time consuming process and must be used in combination with other evidence to construct an accurate picture of a crime. Blood spatter patterns can provide some very important information about:

- The type of weapon used and the velocity of the trauma associated with it

- The number of times a person is struck

- The handedness of the assailant (typically a perpetrator strikes with their dominant hand on the opposite side of the victims body)

- Positions of the victim and perpetrator during and after an attack

- The order in which wounds were inflicted

- The type of injuries that were sustained by the victim and the perpetrator

- The approximate time since the crime was committed

- If death was immediate or occurred over a longer, delayed amount of time

Blood spatter evidence can tell investigators a story about a violent crime that has been committed. Blood follows the laws of gravity and motion; therefore it behaves in a predictable manner which allows for it to be interpreted. Blood molecules are very cohesive (attracted to each other) and thus travel in a uniform spherical shape until they strike a surface or another force acts upon them. Let's look at some of the features that a blood spatter expert looks at to recreate a crime scene.

Surface Texture

The texture of the surface in which blood is landing on at a crime scene is very important to subsequent analysis of blood patterns that are made. The harder and less porous a surface is, the less spattering effect will occur when blood strikes that surface. For instance, blood that lands on glass will show much less spattering effects than blood hitting an article of clothing such as a cotton shirt.

Blood striking a glass surface will not have a large spatter effect.

Speed/Velocity

The velocity of the blood spatter can indicate what type of weapon was used in the crime. The smaller the blood drops, the faster they were moving upon impact. A tiny frosting of droplets is indicative of **high velocity blood spatter** usually as a result of a gunshot wound. Gunshot wounds can have both **back spatter** (bullet entry) and **front spatter** (bullet exit) patterns, or back spatter only if the bullet does not exit the body. Back spatter is usually much smaller than front spatter since front spatter follows the path of the bullet. **Medium velocity spatter** is suggestive of trauma caused by a blunt object such as a bat or fist, but may also be the result of a stabbing with a sharp object. **Low velocity spatter** is usually associated with dripping blood, usually stemming from an injury that has already occurred during an attack. For example, if a victim is stabbed by a knife and then walks around the scene dripping blood from their wounds onto the surrounding surface. This is called **passive spatter**. Low velocity spatter may also be caused by blood dripping from a weapon used to inflict the injury such as a knife.

High velocity spatter is indicative of a gunshot wound.

Direction

The direction that blood strikes an object can be determined by the shape of the blood droplets. Blood that falls at a 90 degree angle to the surface will be spherical in shape with no tail. Blood that strikes an object at any other angle than 90 degrees will have a discernable tail. The orientation of the tail will indicate which direction the blood was traveling when it made the impact. For instance, if the blood droplet tail is oriented to the left the spatter occurred in a right to left direction.

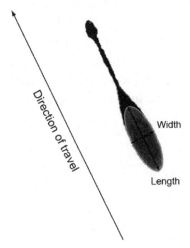

The orientation of the tail of a blood droplet indicates the direction the blood was cast.

Angle of Impact

Blood drops can also provide an investigator with the angle of impact in which a blow occurred to cause an injury. As the angle of impact increases, the more distorted the blood drop becomes, creating a longer tail structure. Thus, the greater the difference between the length and the width of the blood drop, the steeper the angle of impact. Blood spatter experts utilize a mathematical equation: The angle of impact is equal to the arc sin of the drop's width divided by its length ($A = arc\ sin\ (width/length)$). This helps the examiner to begin to determine the original positions of the victim and assailant during an assault.

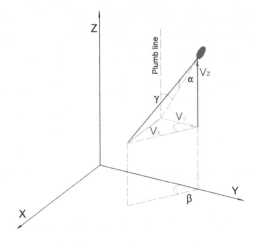

The difference between the length and width of a blood drop indicates its angle of impact.

Origin of Impact

Blood spatter analysis can also provide investigators with the origin of the original impact that was sustained during the crime. Using a representative sample of blood drops from the scene and determining where the angle of each of these drops converges can give an investigator the exact location of a victim when the impact occurred. Were they standing, kneeling, or lying down? Blood spatter experts in the past relied on the "stringing" method to determine the area of convergence. This involved the painstaking task of attaching strings to each spatter mark and bringing them together to find the source of origin. This method is still used occasionally, but has mostly been replaced with a computerized model. Computer programs for crime scene reconstruction create a three-dimensional model of the crime scene by compiling all the lengths and widths of a representative number of blood drops and calculating where they converge. Blood experts can also use small portable lasers at the scene in place of the strings to find the area of convergence.

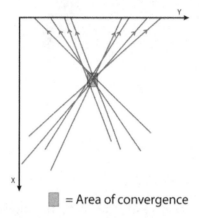

 = Area of convergence

The area of convergence is calculated by compiling all the lengths and widths of a representative number of blood drops from a crime scene.

Summary

Blood spatter analysis can help to reconstruct a crime scene. A blood spatter expert uses the number, shape, and patterns made with blood evidence from a crime to help them determine details of the event. First, they must verify that the substance found is in fact blood and is human in nature. The size, shape, and pattern of blood spatter help to determine the type of weapon used in a crime and the locations of the perpetrator and victim during an assault.

Concept Reinforcement

1. What questions must be answered before a blood spatter expert can conduct an analysis of scene.

2. What type of trauma typically results in high impact spatter patterns?

3. How does a blood spatter expert determine the origin of impact from blood spatter evidence?

Chapter 21 – Impression Evidence

Chapter Objective

- Describe the importance of impression and toolmark evidence in solving a crime

What can impression evidence tell investigators?

Impression evidence occurs when a material or object takes on the form of another object through direct physical contact. The most commonly used impression evidence in criminal cases includes footprints or shoe impressions, tire tread impressions, and tool marks. These types of impressions are used to make physical matches to the original source. For instance, a shoe impression found at a crime scene may be matched to a shoe of the suspected perpetrator of the crime. The matching of impression evidence works similar to fingerprinting analysis and many criminalists specialize in both fingerprint and impression evidence. Impression evidence can be used in a criminal trial to connect a person to a crime. Let's investigate these three common types of impression evidence.

Impression evidence such as footprints are created
through direct physical contact with a surface.

Footprints & Shoeprints

Footprints are similar to fingerprints because they leave remnants of organic substances such as amino acids, proteins, and oils from perspiration. Footprints however are not as unique as fingerprint evidence and are rarely used as a single means of conviction for a crime. Shoeprints on the other hand do not contain organic substances, but are very useful in making comparisons with a suspect's shoes. Shoes can leave either a two or three-dimensional image on a surface that it comes in contact with. Two-dimensional impression images are left on flat surfaces such as wooden floors. When a shoeprint leaves a deep impression mark in the mud or snow, it is three-dimensional in nature. Shoe prints can give an investigator an idea of a perpetrator's height based on the distance between the shoeprints. They can also help tell some of the story from a crime scene such as if a person was standing or running at the scene. Footprint trails can help lead investigators to a secondary crime scene or another set of impression evidence such as tire marks.

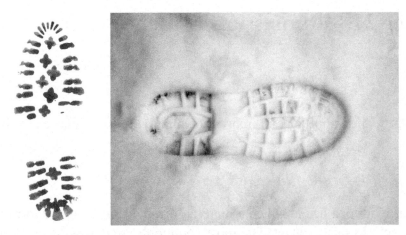

A shoe print left on a solid surface (left) is two-dimensional,
while a shoeprint left in the snow (right) is three-dimensional in nature.

Collecting Shoeprint Evidence

A shoeprint can be either visible or latent (not visible). Visible prints are easy to spot, such as the examples in the photographs above. Latent prints can be found using alternative light sources. Once a likely latent footprint is found, a light dusting of gray or black powder is used to expose the shoe print. The collection of shoeprint evidence at a crime scene is very challenging and requires training and practice. Before a shoeprint is attempted to be preserved, it is photographed extensively to record all of the details in the print. Shoe prints are also photographed relative to their position within the entire crime scene. Photographs give a good idea of orientation, distance between prints (can give an idea of a suspects height), and their relationship to other objects within the scene.

The distance between footprints can give investigators an idea of a perpetrator's height.

Depending on the type of foot print impression, different methods are used to preserve the print. If possible, the entire surface with the print is removed and taken in its original form to the laboratory for analysis. This is not always possible however, therefore techniques for preserving the print are available to use at the scene. Two-dimensional prints that have been exposed are usually preserved using the same lifting technique that is used to lift fingerprints. Many times wider lifting tape is used to accommodate the entire print, but care must be taken to avoid getting air bubbles trapped in the tape which can alter the details of the print. A visible footprint that is made from dirt on the sole of a shoe can be lifted using a different technique known as **electrostatic lifting**. This method involves affixing a sheet of mylar on top of the dusty print and using a roller to smooth it down. Then, an electrostatic unit is run over top of the mylar creating a charge difference and causing the dust to attach to the lifting film underneath. This method works very well for dusty footprints that are barely visible on deep colored surfaces.

The electrostatic lifting machine works similar to the static electricity created when a balloon is rubbed along a person's hair causing it to stand up.

When a shoeprint is three-dimensional in nature, a **cast** or mold of the print is necessary to preserve the details. Casts of footprints provide a significant amount of detail including characteristics of the sides of the shoe in addition to the bottom of the sole. A good casting can be matched to one individual shoe using the enormous amount of preserved detail. Investigators used to use Plaster of Paris, but this has been mostly replaced with dental stone which is easier to work with. If there is water present, a simple casting frame is built around the print and the casting material is poured over the print. The material is allowed to harden and lifted from the scene. It is then sent back to the laboratory for cleaning and analysis. Special formulations such as Snow Print Wax can be used to preserve prints made within the snow. Once a footprint has been preserved, it can then be used for comparison to other samples. The most significant comparisons are those between unique wear patterns on the shoes including cuts, scrapes, or other damage that has a characteristic appearance. A test impression is made with the shoe in question and compared with those preserved from the scene. Impression specialists can also use the **Shoeprint Image Capture and Retrieval System (SICAR)** for comparison if no suspect has been identified. This helps to identify the specific shoe model and can provide a list of vendors that sell that type of shoe.

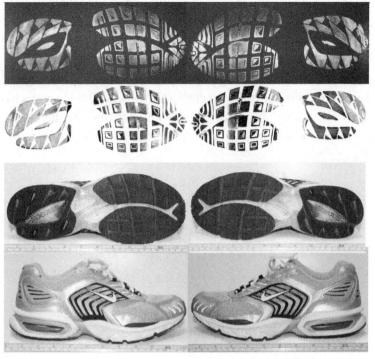

Test impressions may be made of a suspects shoe and
compared to shoeprints found at a scene.

Tire Tread Impressions

When tire marks are found, first an investigator looks for opposite-sided tire marks. This allows a measurement to be made between the impressions, which may provide preliminary information about the make of the car. Tire tracks may also provide information about the mechanics of a car and how fast it was traveling. The details of the tire treads can also provide the style and manufacturer of the tire. Computerized tire data bases can help match tire characteristics to a certain type of tire. The defects and wear on a tire from the road can individualize tires, which can later be matched to one particular car suspected to be involved in a crime. Tire marks found at a scene are photographed extensively and then preserved through the same casting methods as three-dimensional footprints.

Tire tread impressions can provide information about the model of a car and
individual characteristics of the tire treads which can be matched to a specific car.

Tool Marks

A **tool mark** is an impression that is formed when a tool comes in contact with a surface creating gouges, cuts, or abrasions to the surface. For instance, a suspect may use a crowbar, wire cutter, or screwdriver to pry their way into a window or door. This leaves distinct marks on the surface and can act as a type of "fingerprint" for a certain tool. Tool marks are typically in one of two forms: **friction marks** or **stamping marks**. Friction marks occur when a part of a tool rubs against a surface. Stamp marks create a full impression of the edge of a tool. Many times impressions are a combination of the two types of marks. Sometimes a door frame is removed and taken to the lab to study tool marks that are left after a crime. Other times casts are created at the scene and can be compared to specific tools found at the scene or in the possession of a suspect. Tool marks are photographed before they are casted. Any tools that are suspected to match the markings are bagged in order to preserve any trace evidence on the surface. When impressions from tool marks are studied at a higher magnification, distinct markings can be matched to a specific tool. These microscopic matches are from a tools random nicks and scratches caused by wear and tear. **Comparison microscopes** are used to line up markings found at a scene with a sample of markings from a suspected tool.

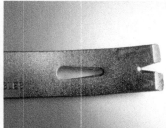

Tool marks made during a criminal act can be casted and matched to a tool using individual characteristics made from the wear and tear on a specific tool.

Summary

Impression evidence occurs when a material or object takes the form of another object through direct physical contact. This includes footprints, shoe prints, tire marks, and tool marks. These impressions can be preserved and compared to other samples for a suspected match. The preservation of impression evidence is done through a variety of methods depending on the type of impression. Lifting tape can be used to preserve two-dimensional impressions, while casting can be used to create a mold of three-dimensional impressions. Impression evidence that is matched through a comparison microscope to a suspected shoe, tire, or tool can be used as evidence in a criminal trial.

Concept Reinforcement

1. What are the three common types of impression evidence?

2. How is a three-dimensional shoe print preserved for later analysis?

3. How are tool marks matched to a suspected tool?

Chapter 22 – Trace Evidence

Chapter Objective

- Describe the importance of trace evidence in understanding the crime scene

What is trace evidence?

"Every contact leaves a trace" was the motto coined by Edmond Locard, a famous criminologist in the mid-1900s. This is still true in crime scene investigation today as criminals always leave traces of themselves at the scene of a crime. **Trace evidence** is left due to the contact of objects or substances with one another through contact friction. The most commonly collected trace evidence includes hairs, glass, paint chips/flecks, fibers, dirt/dust/soil, plant materials, and explosive chemicals. Sometimes other evidence is classified as trace evidence including firearms, ammunition, blood, body fluids, bite marks, tire impressions, shoeprints, tool marks, rope, duct tape pieces, etc. When samples are collected of any of these types of evidence they are sent to the crime laboratory for thorough analysis. Many times the labs will have criminalists that specialize in certain forms of trace evidence. Let's take a look at four of the most common types of trace evidence and what they can tell an investigator.

Hair

- Hair can be collected from a crime scene in several different ways:

- Collection of visible hair at the scene by gloved hand. Many times tweezers can damage the structure of hair if they are used in the collection process.

- Infrared or laser lighting is used to find difficult to see hairs at the scene.

- Lifting tape may be used to pick up both visible and non-visible hair samples.

- Vacuums can be used to pick up hair into specialized filters. These are extremely useful when a large area is involved.

- The brushing/scraping/shaking of a garment suspected to contain trace evidence over a white sheet of paper.

- Garments and other materials may be placed in a bag and agitated followed by the collection of trace evidence at the bottom of the bag.

- Combing or clipping of hair for instance in a rape case the pubic hair is combed to look for hair from the perpetrator.

Hair consists of an inner **cortex** and **medulla** surrounded by a protective layer called the **cuticle.** The cuticle consists of overlapping scales that extend outward in the direction of the hair growth. Hair is enclosed by a hair follicle and grows from a point of origin called the **papilla.** It consists of dead, cornified cells. The part of the hair contained underneath the skin is called the **root** and the area that projects out from the skin is termed the **shaft**. Pigment granules within the cortex and medulla determine the coloration of the hair.

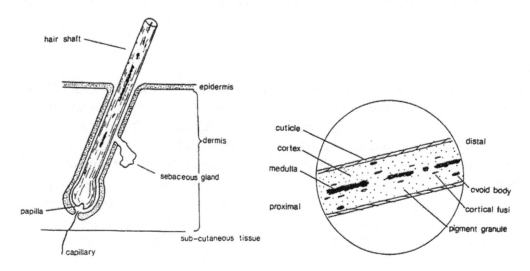

Cross sections of a hair follicle (left) and an individual hair (right).

Hair evidence collected at a scene is examined under a microscope and can tell investigators many different things. From looking at the root of a hair, a criminalist can tell if it fell out naturally or was pulled out. Hair examination can reveal if the hair is in fact human or from another animal species. The hair root may contain DNA that can be used for comparison purposes later on. For instance, hair found on a knife or other murder weapon may be matched to the victim of an assault. A side-by-side microscopic comparison can also be made between a suspect's hair and a hair found at a crime scene to link them to the crime. Hair analysis can also indicate the racial origin of the owner, hair coloration, and length of the hair. These can help to create a profile of a suspect. Finally, hair can also be tested in suspected causes of poisoning by a toxicologist. Since hair remains long after the flesh on a body has decomposed, it remains a viable source of evidence for a very long time.

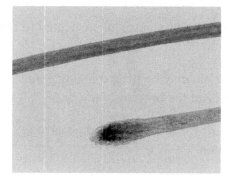

Microscopic photograph of a hair root

Concept Extension: Napoleon Bonaparte

Napoleon Bonaparte was the emperor of France in the early 1800s. He was imprisoned and exiled to an island in the Mid-Atlantic and died in 1821. Rumors were that he was poisoned to death by his English captors, but there was no way to prove it at the time. Napoleon stated his suspicions in his diary entries saved by his valet at the time. His valet also saved a lock of his hair as a memento. With the development of new hair analysis technology in the 20th century, the saved hair was analyzed and revealed high levels of arsenic. The hair shaft was suggestive of high doses of arsenic administered over the four months preceding his death. Who exactly poisoned Napoleon may never be known.

Napoleon Bonaparte

Glass

Glass fragments discovered at a crime scene can tell crime scene investigators a story about certain aspects of a crime. The following are some examples of what a glass expert may be able to discern from the analysis of glass fragments collected from a scene:

- Fragments of glass from an automobile accident can be embedded in a victim's hair or clothing and be matched to a vehicle in a hit and run.

- Auto glass can be matched to narrow down the possible type of vehicle involved in a crash.

- The direction of the impact can be determined by examining the glass shards. This can show if the glass was broken from the inside or outside of a building or car.

- Glass shards found on a potential robbery suspect can be matched to broken glass at the scene.

- Examination of glass shards can determine the velocity of impact sustained to cause the damage such as a low-impact from a fist or a high-impact from a bullet.

It's important to collect as many pieces of glass from a scene as possible to provide the best reconstruction possible. Criminalists who specialize in glass evidence reassemble the pieces and analyze the story they tell. Glass can be classified using the refractive index to match it to a specific type of glass. **Spectrography** may also be used to analyze glass fragments by utilizing a specialized machine called a spectrograph.

Glass can be used to link a suspect or a car to a crime scene.

Paint

Paint is one of the favorite pieces of evidence for trace evidence specialists because of the ability to match it so distinctly with its source. The irregularities on the edges of a paint chip can be matched to a piece of furniture, a specific tool, or a vehicle. Auto paint is particularly helpful in hit and run accidents to help identify the model and make of the suspected car. Auto paint is applied in layers. The topcoat helps investigators identify the color of the car by matching it to manufacturer samples. The undercoat makes it possible to narrow down the possibilities to a specific model, the plant in which it was manufactured, and which dealership it was delivered to.

Paint chips found at the scene of a hit and run accident can be matched to a specific car.

Fibers

Fiber evidence can be found in a variety of different ways at a crime scene. For instance, the contact made between a perpetrator and victim may allow a cross-transfer of fiber from clothing items to occur. This fiber evidence can be collected from either the perpetrator or the victim of the crime and matched to one another. Fibers may also adhere to pieces of glass during a break in or to a vehicle during a hit-and-run accident. Fibers can either be natural or synthetic (man-made) in nature. A **comparison microscope** is used to identify particular fibers found at a scene. Natural and synthetic fibers have a very different appearance under the microscope. Synthetic fibers have a smooth and regular consistency in their external appearance, while natural fibers are more irregular with a more detailed internal structure. Criminalists use fiber catalogues to identify a fiber type by matching certain characteristics such as fiber diameter, cross-sectional shape, length, and color. Fibers that are collected at a scene or on a victim can be matched under a microscope to fibers collected at a suspect's house, car trunk, or other location. Fiber evidence can then be used in court during a criminal trial.

Fiber evidence can be collected and studied under the microscope for identification.

Summary

Trace evidence is left at the scene of a crime through the friction contact between objects or substances. The most common types of trace evidence include hair, glass, paint, and fibers. Trace evidence is collected from a scene and sent to a criminal laboratory for analysis. The matching of trace evidence from a crime scene to a suspected perpetrator of a crime can be used in a criminal trial to establish a link between them.

Concept Reinforcement

1. What is trace evidence?

2. What can the examination of hair evidence at scene tell investigators?

3. What tool do criminalists use to compare and analyze fiber evidence?

Chapter 23 – Ballistic and Firearm Evidence

Chapter Objectives

- Describe the importance of ballistic and firearm evidence in building a criminal case

Firearms Identification

Firearms and **ballistics** (analysis of bullets and bullet impacts) evidence are very important components in solving violent crimes in the US. This is because many of the violent crimes in the US are committed with firearms. As a result, the evidence gathered from firearms is critical to solving the crimes and prosecuting the criminals. Firearms identification involves much more than just the bullet comparisons shown on TV crime dramas. A specialist working in the discipline of firearms identification must have extensive knowledge of how all types of weapons are constructed and operated. Aside from making comparisons of bullets and casings found at a scene, a firearms specialist also participates in the following important tasks:

- Restoration of obscured serial numbers

- Detection of gunpowder residues on garments and surrounding wounds

- Estimation of distance between gun and target during firing of a weapon

- Detection of gunpowder residues on hands of suspected shooters

Bullet Comparison

The barrel of a gun is a solid bar of steel with a hollow center. The center is hollowed out using specialized drills. These drills leave distinctive markings on each gun that is made. During the gun making process, a step called **rifling** involves the impressing of the inner surface of the barrel with spiral **grooves**. Surrounding these sunken grooves are raised areas called **lands**. As a bullet is fired from a gun, it travels along and spins under the guidance of the grooves within the barrel. Each firearm manufacturer uses a certain rifling process, giving the firearm examiner the ability to distinguish one brand of firearm from another based on the pattern of lands and grooves. Within the barrel of the gun, there are also unique markings called **striations** that are left there due to the unique minute imperfections found within a rifling tool. These striations are random and irregular, making it impossible for two gun barrels to have the same markings. Striations make it

A bullet can be matched to a specific gun based on the rifling characteristics of the barrel.

possible for investigators to match a bullet to a specific firearm. As a bullet passes through the barrel of a gun, its surface is impressed with the rifled markings of the barrel. The lands and grooves found on a bullet can identify the type of firearm used and the striations can match a specific gun to the bullet. When a gun is found, the examiner fires a test round and makes a comparison between the test bullet and the bullet collected from the scene of the crime. This is done using a comparison microscope.

Cartridge Cases

The bullet from a crime scene is not the only useful piece of evidence in linking the crime to a specific gun. When a weapon is fired, the trigger results in the firing pin striking against the primer, this causes the ignition of a powder and the propulsion of a bullet through the barrel. Once the bullet is fired, the **casing/shell** or **cartridge case** is expelled backward against the breechblock (rear aspect of the firearm). The cartridge case is impressed with the markings of the weapon's firing and loading mechanisms. These markings found on collected cartridge cases at a crime scene can be compared to a recovered weapon at the scene. A test firing of the weapon is conducted, and the individual casing marks are compared under a microscope to determine if there is a match.

Bullet cartridge cases can be matched to a specific gun used in a crime.

What happens if the firearm is not recovered?

Sometimes the police are unable to recover the weapon used in a crime. It is still possible to solve crimes using firearm evidence even if the weapon is not available. The US Bureau of Alcohol, Tobacco and Firearms (ATF) maintain the IBIS database. The Integrated Ballistics Identification System is a database of ammunition including expended bullets and cartridge cases. Investigators use IBIS to match bullets or cartridge cases from crime scenes to bullets or casings found at other crime scenes. This allows investigators to make connections between multiple crime scenes and to develop theories surrounding each of the crimes. This can help with the apprehension of suspects and eventual convictions more likely to occur.

Gunpowder Residues

Every weapon does not eject spent cartridges (i.e. shotguns), but they all release **gunshot residue (GSR)** when they are fired. GSR is composed of a cloud of vapors and particulates that contains several chemicals such as lead, barium, and antimony. The presence and pattern of GSR on garments collected from the victim can tell investigators the approximate distance between a shooter and victim during the commission of a crime. When the muzzle of a weapon is close enough to a target, the GSR products are deposited onto the target. The pattern of the residue around a bullet hole can give an approximate estimate of the distance from which a weapon was fired. When a target is over 3 feet away, no powder is typically deposited onto the target. The determination of distance between a shooter and a victim can help to verify the story of eyewitnesses, including the shooter.

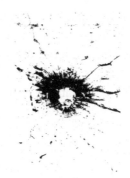

The presence and pattern of GSR on garments from a shooting victim can help to determine the distance between a shooter and the victim.

When a weapon is fired, gunshot residue (GSR) is not just expelled toward the victim, but also backwards toward the shooter. This result in traces of GSR being displaced onto the shooters hands. The most common areas for GSR are the web area of the thumb and the back of the shooting hand. Testing for the presence of GSR on a suspects hand can tell investigators if a person has fired a weapon recently or was in proximity to a weapon that has been fired. People can also get GSR on their hands by handling a weapon that has been recently fired. The most popular method used by examiner's to test for the presence of GSR is the application of adhesive tape over the area to collect any residue. The tape is then tested at the crime lab for GSR. The presence of GSR on a suspects hand alone is not enough to convict a person of a crime, but it does provide supportive evidence in a criminal trial.

GSR is deposited on the hand of the shooter as a weapon is discharged.

Serial Number Restoration

Serial numbers are stamped onto the metal frame or body of weapons with solid steel dies. The dies are punched into the frame with a great degree of force to embed the numbers at a certain depth. Serial numbers of weapons are registered to the owner of a weapon when it is purchased. Many times criminals try to file off or degrade serial numbers from a weapon so that they cannot be traced to a particular person. A firearms expert can restore a serial number that a criminal has attempted to destroy by applying an etching agent. The etching agent dissolves faster within the impressions created by the serial numbers which allows the chain of numbers to be revealed after the agent is added.

Collection of Firearms Evidence

Firearm evidence should be treated like any other physical evidence at a crime scene. It must be carefully collected and marked to preserve the chain of custody. Weapons that are collected are tagged around the trigger guard and include the initials of the investigator who collected the evidence. A weapon should not be cleaned or wiped off in any way and transported in the condition that it is found. Safety precautions must be taken in case a weapon is loaded. Most times a weapon is unloaded before the transfer is made. The bullets which are unloaded are individually tagged and marked with their corresponding locations in the weapon. If it cannot be unloaded, the weapon is carried within a bulletproof case. Care must be taken when collecting a firearm so that no trace evidence (i.e. fingerprints, fibers) is lost that may be present on the weapon. Bullets and cartridges that are collected at the scene must also be collected with care to avoid making any marks on the metal that could disrupt the striations that are present. The clothing of a firearms victim is also carefully preserved so that possible patterns of GSR are not disrupted before examination.

Firearm evidence must be carefully collected and examined to avoid disturbing trace evidence and striation markings.

Summary

Firearms and ballistics evidence are very important components of criminal investigations. A firearms specialist must be familiar with the construction and functioning of every type of weapon. They are responsible for making comparisons between bullets or casings found at a crime scene and a suspected weapon. Firearm experts are also responsible for the detection of gunshot residue (GSR) on a victim's clothing or the hands of a suspected shooter. This can tell investigator's the approximate distance between a shooter and victim or if a person has fired a weapon recently. Finally, the firearms expert is involved in the restoration of serial numbers that can be used to identify the owner of the weapon. Firearm and ballistics evidence must be collected from a crime scene with extreme care to avoid destroying trace evidence or unique patterns of striations.

Concept Reinforcement

1. What are the main roles of a firearms expert?

2. What is used to make comparisons between a bullet from a crime scene and a test bullet fired from a suspected gun?

3. What can the presence of GSR tell investigators about a crime?

Chapter 24 – Forensic Serology

Chapter Objective

• Describe the importance of serology analysis in solving a crime

What is serology?

Serology is the study of blood, semen, saliva, or other bodily fluids using the detection of specific **antigens** and enzymes. Serology techniques are most often used to identify seminal or saliva stains, or for the typing of blood stains found at a scene. In this section, we will focus on the most common procedure conducted in a general serology laboratory, blood typing.

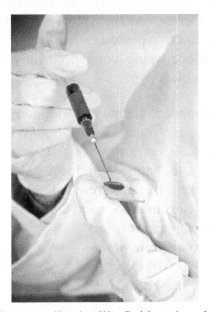

Serology studies bodily fluid such as blood
by identifying specific antigens and enzymes.

Human Blood Type Basics

Human blood is composed of a mixture of specialized cells, enzymes, proteins, and other inorganic substances. The fluid part of the blood is called the **plasma** which is mostly composed of water. Within the plasma, the solid aspects of blood are suspended throughout. The main cell types of the blood are the red blood cells, white blood cells, and platelets. If the solid components of the blood are filtered out, a pale yellow-colored liquid is left called **serum**. In the forensic world, the most pertinent aspects of blood are the red blood cells and serum which we will focus on in this section.

The blood contains red blood cells, white blood cells, and platelets suspended in liquid plasma.

The red blood cells are responsible for the transport of oxygen from the lungs to the bodily tissues. They also are involved in the removal of carbon dioxide waste from the tissues and transportation back to the lungs where is can be exhaled. Red blood cells also possess specialized chemical structures called **antigens** on their surface. These antigens are what determine a person's blood type. Over fifteen blood-antigen groupings have been discovered, however the most commonly used are the ABO and Rh systems. There are four possible blood types in the **ABO system**: A, B, AB, and O types. A person with type A blood possesses A antigens on the surface of their red blood cells, while a person with type B blood has B antigens on the surface instead. AB blood types contain both A and B antigens on the surface of the red blood cells and O blood types do not have either A or B antigens on their surface. The **Rh system** is simpler and can be either positive or negative in type. An Rh positive person possesses the D antigen, while an Rh negative person does not have the D antigen. Blood typing looks specifically for the A, B, and D antigens in order to classify an individual's blood type.

The blood serum is also an important component of blood in relationship to blood typing procedures in the laboratory. Serum contains specialized proteins called **antibodies** which are the counterparts to specific antigens. Every antigen has a corresponding antibody and is named accordingly. For instance, the antibody for the A antigen is called the anti-A antibody. The anti-A antibody will only react with the corresponding A antigen. The serum that contains certain antibodies is called **anti-serum** and is used to test for specific blood types. When an antibody reacts with its specific antigen it causes a clumping effect to occur called **agglutination**. For example, a blood sample that is type A will possess anti-B antibodies, but not anti-A antibodies. This results in a clumping effect when exposed to anti-B serum and no clumping when it is combined with anti-A serum. These effects are what tell a serologist the blood type of a specific sample. This same procedure is used to test for the presence or absence of the D antigen to identify if a person is Rh positive or negative. Look at the table below to see how the ABO blood type is revealed through the use of anti-serums to detect specific antigens.

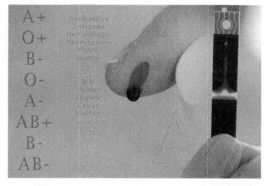

The process of blood typing involves looking for the A, B, and D antigens.

Blood Type (ABO)	A-Antigen Present	B-Antigen Present	Anti-A Antibody Present	Anti-B Antibody Present
A	Yes	No	No	Yes
B	No	Yes	Yes	No
AB	Yes	Yes	No	No
O	No	No	Yes	Yes

The antigens and antibodies present in the ABO blood types.

What is the purpose of blood typing in forensics?

The process of determining the blood type of a sample collected at a scene is relatively simple and inexpensive. Blood type cannot be individually matched to one individual, but it can be used as a means to eliminate suspects. For instance, if a blood sample of a suspect is determined to be type B and the sample from the crime scene is type AB (a sample that is suspected to have come from the perpetrator of the crime), there is no way that the sample could have come from that suspect. On the other hand, if the blood type of the suspect is also AB, there is a good chance that it could have originated with that suspect and further testing should be initiated. Blood typing is a good screening tool to determine if more expensive DNA testing methods should be done to obtain an individual match.

Summary

Serology is the study of blood, semen, saliva, or other bodily fluids using the detection of specific antigens and enzymes. One of the most common tests done in the serology lab is blood typing using the ABO and Rh systems. The serologist uses antiserums containing specific antibodies which react with certain antigens. When an antibody reacts with its specific antigen it causes a clumping effect called agglutination. This tells the serologist the blood type of a sample. Blood typing can be used to eliminate suspects or to suggest further testing when the blood types are a match between a suspect and sample.

. . . .

Concept Reinforcement

1. What are the two most common blood grouping systems used for blood typing in serology?

2. What type of antigens and antibodies would a person with type A blood have?

3. What can blood typing be using for in forensic settings?

Chapter 25 – DNA Fingerprinting

Chapter Objective

- Describe the importance of DNA fingerprinting and CODIS

DNA and Forensics

DNA (deoxyribonucleic acid) is the genetic material contained within all the cells of the body that contain a nucleus. This includes white blood cells, semen, tooth pulp, hair roots, and waste cells of the saliva or urine. Red blood cells do not contain a nucleus; therefore they do not have DNA. A molecule of DNA appears microscopically like a twisted ladder otherwise known as a double helix. Each side of the ladder is made up of alternating phosphates and sugars (deoxyribose sugar). The rungs of the ladder are composed of pairs of nucleotide bases called **adenine (A), guanine (G), thymine (T),** and **cytosine (C).** Adenine only pairs with thymine and guanine only pairs with cytosine. Human DNA contains approximately 3 billion of these paired rungs. When a cell divides during replication, the DNA ladder unzips and each half acts as a model for the formation of a new strand of DNA. A **gene** is made up of a specific group of nucleotides that provide the instructions for building a specific protein. All the genes together determine an individual's physical characteristics such as eye color, skin color, blood type, etc. No two people aside from identical twins have the same DNA sequence. An example of a DNA sequence could be:

ATACGTTTACGTATCATTACGA

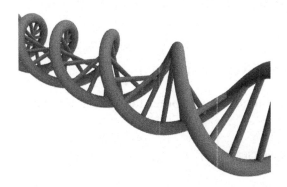

The DNA molecule is structured similar to a twisted ladder.

DNA Fingerprinting

One of the most significant developments in forensics was the advent of **DNA fingerprinting**. DNA fingerprinting allows a scientist to match a DNA sample to a specific individual. In order to create a DNA fingerprint from a sample, a common technique called **STR (short tandem repeats)** is utilized. STRs are locations on the gene sequence that repeat themselves a number of times. The number of times these sequences repeat vary among each individual, which creates a individualized "genetic fingerprint". DNA analysts use 13 different STRs for comparison purposes when attempting to make a match. When a sample is analyzed, **restriction enzymes** are used to cut the DNA at specified sites and then amplified (copied multiple times) through a process called **PCR (polymerase chain reaction).** The STRs are then separated onto a gel through another process called **electrophoresis**. Depending on the size of the fragments, a distinct pattern of banding is created that can be compared to a reference sample of a suspect. DNA evidence provides a definitive test for scientists to identify or exonerate a suspect in question.

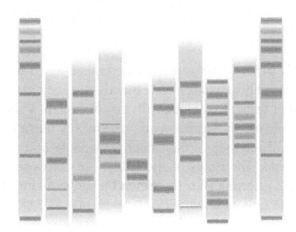

DNA fingerprinting compares the DNA of samples based on the size of specific fragments of DNA. These create unique banding patterns like those seen above.

Collection of DNA Samples

Before a DNA sample can be collected, it needs to be found. Chemicals such as luminol and alternative light sources like UV light can be used to help investigators find DNA at a crime scene. Some common sources of DNA evidence include:

- Fingernails

- Paper products (paper towels, tissues, etc.)

- Toothpicks, cigarette butts, and any other items that may have come in contact with the mouth

- Linens (sheets, pillowcases, etc.)

- Glasses or contact lenses

- Seal of an envelope or on a used stamp

- Ligatures (rope, cords, tape)

When a DNA sample is collected, care must be taken to avoid contamination to the sample. Crime scene investigators use gloves to collect evidence and disposable tools to prevent the transfer of evidence. Samples can be degraded if they are exposed to direct sunlight, extreme humidity, or bacterial growth; therefore cooled containers are used to transport and store DNA evidence.

Investigators must take precautions to avoid the contamination of DNA evidence during collection.

DNA and CODIS

Beginning in 1998, local, state, and federal agencies have compiled databases of DNA profiles. Similar to the fingerprint database, AFIS, the **Combined DNA Index System (CODIS)** stores 13 specified STR points of convicted criminals. The Federal DNA identification Act of 1994 restricts the database to the DNA of convicted criminals, including sex offenders. Access is granted to law enforcement personnel only and requires a court order to be used during a criminal trial. DNA samples found at a crime scene can be analyzed and submitted into CODIS for comparison. Many repeat offenders have been identified using this sophisticated database.

DNA samples of convicted criminals are stored in a database known as CODIS.

Summary

DNA or deoxyribonucleic acid is the genetic material present in all body cells containing a nucleus. The DNA sequence of all individuals with the exception of identical twins is unique. The process of DNA fingerprinting can be used to match a DNA sample found at a crime scene to a specific suspect. Crime scene investigators must take adequate precautions when collecting suspected DNA samples from a scene to avoid contamination. The STRs, or short tandem repeats, from 13 different locations on the DNA of convicted criminals are stored in a federal database known as CODIS. This database can compare samples from a crime scene and identify repeat offenders.

Concept Reinforcement

1. Briefly explain the structure of DNA.

2. Why must care be taken during the processing of DNA collection at a crime scene?

3. What is CODIS?

Chapter 26 – Forensic Toxicology

Chapter Objective

- Describe forensic toxicology and its applications

Forensic Toxicology

Forensic toxicology is involved in the detection and identification of drugs and/or poisons in the body fluids, tissues, and organs. This can include testing urine, blood, saliva, hair, fingernails, or other tissue samples from the body. Forensic toxicologists have advanced training in analytical chemistry and pharmacology to help aid in the investigation of death related to suspected poisonings or drug usage. This requires a thorough knowledge of how different types of substances are metabolized in the body. The toxicologist uses information and samples collected from the scene of a crime to help them identify the presence of toxic substances. This can include empty pill bottles, powders, trace residues, or other chemicals present at the scene. This can give a toxicologist a place to begin investigating for the presence of a suspicious substance.

Forensic toxicology is concerned with the detection and
identification of drugs and/or poisons.

Alcohol

One of the most common tests conducted within the toxicology lab is for **blood alcohol level**. Alcohol is a central nervous system depressant that primarily affects the brain. Alcohol appears in the blood within minutes after ingestion and increases slowly in concentration as it is absorbed into the body tissues. Once a maximum alcohol level is reached, the level begins to decline until it completely dissipates. The rate of alcohol absorption and dissipation varies depending on a person's age, weight, and physical condition. Police officers use breath analysis when a person is suspected of driving under the influence. If they are found to be over the legal limit, they are taken for a more accurate blood sample to determine the blood alcohol level. In the United States, a blood alcohol concentration over .08 percent is considered over the legal intoxication limit.

The most common toxicology test is for blood-alcohol concentration. Police use breath analysis as a means to screen for possible intoxication levels over the legal limit. A breathalyzer device is pictured above.

Poisons

For many centuries poisons were a commonly undetected method of murder. Toxicology testing simply did not exist; therefore there was no proof to establish murder. Today poisonings are relatively rare; however they do still occur on occasion. The most commonly used poisons are heavy metals such as arsenic, bismuth, antimony, mercury, or thallium. Tests for the presence of heavy metal poisons can be conducted on body fluids by dissolving them into a solution of hydrochloric acid and inserting a copper strip into the solution. If a silvery or dark coating appears on the copper strip, there is a heavy metal poison present. Tests can also be carried out on hair and fingernail samples long after death has occurred. The most common poison encountered in the toxicology lab is **carbon monoxide (CO).** CO is responsible for many accidental deaths and suicides every year. When CO enters the bloodstream in large quantities, it blocks the ability of hemoglobin to carry oxygen to the tissues resulting in suffocation.

For many centuries poisons were an undetectable means of murder.

Concept Extension: The debut of Toxicology

Marie Capelle was married at the age of 23 against her wishes to a middle-aged, bankrupt iron master named Charles LaFarge in August of 1839. She was seen buying rat poison to kill the rats in their home several days before she brought a homemade cake to her husband at work. He become extremely ill and was sent to the hospital. Servants saw her feeding him with her own hands and his family became suspicious of Marie. Charles died soon after, and Marie was arrested on the charge of murder. When the trial began, the prosecution was disappointed when a new testing method failed to show arsenic in Charles LaFarges stomach. They did find arsenic in food samples taken from around the home, but needed to show the body had significant levels of arsenic in it to kill the deceased. Mathieu Orfila ran the new toxicology test for arsenic in the proper way and demonstrated that Charles did indeed have toxic level of arsenic in his system. This was the first case that successfully used toxicology to convict a suspected murderer.

Marie LaFarge was the first person to be convicted of
murder based on toxicology evidence.

Summary

Forensic toxicology is concerned with the detection and identification of drugs and/or poisons in a medical-legal investigation. Forensic toxicologists have advanced training in the areas of analytical chemistry and pharmacology. The most common test performed in the toxicology laboratory is for blood-alcohol concentration. Toxicologists are also involved in testing for poisons in the system that may have resulted in death.

Concept Reinforcement

1. What is the main role of forensic toxicology?

2. What is the most commonly performed test in the toxicology laboratory?

3. What is the most common poison that is encountered in the toxicology laboratory?

Chapter 27 – Arson/Explosives Investigation

Chapter Objective

- Describe the importance of arson/explosives investigations

Arson/Explosives

Explosions and fires are similar chemical phenomenons. An explosion is typically followed by a fire and many fires lead to explosions. According to the US Fire Administration, there are over 4,000 explosion-related incidents reported every year in the United States alone. **Arson** is considered the purposeful act of starting a fire or explosion in order to do harm to a person, multiple persons, or property. Investigations following a fire or explosion can be extremely difficult and tedious in nature. These types of investigations require the assistance of arson or explosive experts trained for many years and very sophisticated equipment for evidence collection.

Explosions and fires have similar chemical mechanisms.

Investigation of a Fire/Explosion

The investigation of a fire, explosion, or bomb scene requires strict attention to detail and an experienced, well-trained investigator. The first and most important aspect of an explosion/fire investigation is to make sure the scene is safe and secure for personnel to process. The threat of secondary explosions either intentional or as a result of fire must be considered before any other specialists enter the scene. Once the scene has been cleared and an initial walk-through is conducted to determine its size, a 3-dimensional grid pattern is established. After the grid pattern is established, investigators are assigned to a particular area of the grid to document and preserve all evidence present. Evidence can include:

- Probable primary bomb components

- Possible bomb-making components (wires, molding, batteries, etc.)

- Swabs of all surfaces to test for chemical residues

- Evidence of probable placement of victims prior to explosion

A thorough investigator records any evidence of blast patterns, provides preliminary assessments of a possible explosion mechanism, and preserves all relevant trace evidence left at the scene. The investigation many times requires the use of sophisticated equipment such as vapor detectors, GPS units, and trace explosive collectors. Sometimes highly trained arson dogs are used to reveal the presence of accelerants which can suggest the fire or explosion was the result of arson. Once all the data from a scene has been compiled, it is entered into two major reporting authorities including the **FBI Bomb database** and the **ATF Arson and Explosives National Repository**. These databases compare similar mechanisms and preferences among explosion events and can help investigators link several crimes to one perpetrator.

The patterns associated with a particular explosion or fire are entered into a database which can help investigators link several similar crimes to one perpetrator.

The mind of an arsonist or bomber

Bombers and arsonists are typically indiscriminate killers. They may have a specific target in mind, but are not concerned with injuring or killing others that are complete strangers. Many times there is no intended target, just the desire to set fires or explosions. There may even be political or personal reasons behind the attacks that are not well understood by others. Timothy McVeigh, for instance, detonated an explosion in the Oklahoma Federal Building killing government workers and many of the children being cared for in the daycare center that day. Although the children had nothing to do with the government, he did not have the capacity to differentiate between killing them or others that he blamed for his problems.

McVeigh was a United States Army Veteran and a security guard that was opposed to what he viewed as a tyrannical government. The bombing occurred on the second anniversary of the 1993 Waco massacre in which four federal agents and sixth followers of the radical leader David Koresh were killed. Another interesting feature that many arsonists or bombers share is their frequent revisiting of the scene of the crime after it has been committed. Many times they are spotted at the scene watching emergency personnel and sometimes even offer help to the workers during the aftermath. This explains why there are typically extra personnel assigned to the scene to videotape the spectators. These tapes can be reviewed in order to identify possible suspects.

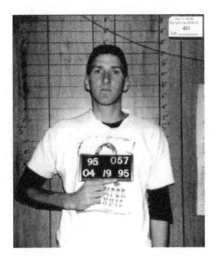

Timothy McVeigh was convicted and executed for the April 1995 bombing of the Oklahoma Federal Building killing 168 people and injuring many others.

Summary

Explosions and fires have similar chemical mechanisms or actions. Arson is considered a deliberate act of setting a fire or explosive to do harm to a person, multiple persons, or property. The investigation of a fire, explosion, or bomb scene requires highly trained personnel with acute attention to detail. Bombers or arsonists are typically indiscriminate killers and many times do not have a specific target associated with their destructive rage.

Concept Reinforcement

1. What is arson?

2. What databases are used to store information concerning arson or bomb-related crimes?

3. What are some common features associated with arsonists or bombers?

Chapter 28 – Organic Analysis Technology

Chapter Objective

- Describe the use of technology in performing organic analysis

Organic Analysis

Forensic scientists are commonly called upon to analyze and identify **organic substances**. An organic substance contains carbon in combination with other elements such as hydrogen, oxygen, nitrogen, phosphorus, or chlorine. In contrast, an inorganic substance is not structurally based on carbon. Once an analyst determines that a substance is organic in nature, they must decide which technique to utilize for the analysis procedure. Analytical techniques can be used as a qualitative or quantitative procedure. Qualitative analyses are only concerned with the identification of a material, while quantitative procedures look at the specific percentage amounts of components contained within a mixture. For example, a qualitative analysis may identify a substance as heroin, but a quantitative procedure will determine how much pure heroin is contained in the sample. The two most common techniques used by a forensic scientist for the identification of organic materials are chromatography and mass spectrometry. Analysts are called upon to identify samples from environmental, biological, and synthetic samples collected at a crime scene. For example, they may test for the presence of commonly abused drugs such as alcohol, marijuana, or amphetamines.

Organic substances contain carbon such as the methane molecule shown above.

Chromatography

Chromatography is a common technique used to purify substances that contain multiple components. Many times impure samples come into the lab and need to be separated for identification purposes. For instance, street drugs are typically diluted by dealers with other substances to make a larger volume of product to sell. Chromatography techniques allow the scientist to first separate the mixture into components. There are several different types of chromatography but they all use two basic phases: a stationary phase and a mobile phase. During the stationary phase a material is used to absorb all the components of the mixture and during the mobile phase all the components are soluble. As the mobile phase moves through the stationary phase, the different components within the mixture are absorbed at different rates and thus are separated. Chromatography techniques include **paper chromatography**,

thin-layer chromatography (TLC), and **gas chromatography (GC)**. Paper chromatography utilizes filter paper as the stationary phase, while thin-layer chromatography uses a thin layer of aluminum oxide on a glass plate. These two processes involve dipping the lower end of the stationary phase into a solvent. The solvent moves up the stationary phase (i.e. filter paper) until it reaches the top. The paper or plate is then dried and the separated spots are analyzed for identification. Gas chromatography is used to separate mixtures of either liquids or solids. The stationary phase is a coating of fine clay or glass beads that are packed into a steel tube. The mixture to be analyzed is the mobile phase and is blown through the tube by another gas (typically nitrogen). Specialized detectors are used to measure the components of the mixture.

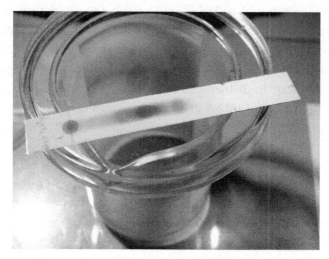

An example of thin-layer chromatography done on a sample of black ink.

Mass Spectrophotometry

The **mass spectrophotometer (mass spec)** is a very complex piece of equipment used in forensic science for chemical analysis. Once a mixture is separated by chromatography, the mass spec can identify extremely small quantities of substances present within the mixture. The sample that is being analyzed is hit with a beam of electrons produced by heating up a wire cathode. This causes the molecules within the sample to break into small electrically charged fragments. These fragments are passed through the spectrophotometer into an electric field causing them to accelerate. Then the fragments move quickly through a magnetic field causing them to deflect away from the straight pathway into a circular pattern. The radius of the circular pathway varies according to the mass of each individual fragment piece (heavy fragments have a larger radius than lighter ones). A detector on the other side produces a spectrum of the different fragments with different intensities. The intensity levels demonstrate the amount of a particular component. These patterns are unique to different chemical structures and can then easily be identified by a computer connected to the mass spec machine.

A mass spec machine used to identify components in a given sample.

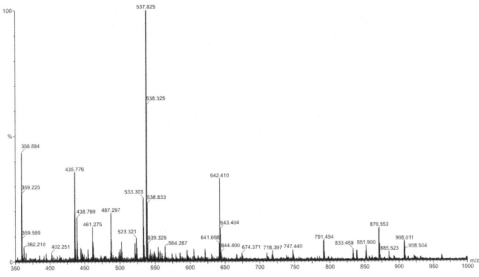

A sample of a mass spec analysis print out.

Summary

Forensic scientists are often responsible for the analysis and identification of organic substances. Organic substances contain carbon within their molecules. Organic analysis can be qualitative or quantitative in nature. The two most common procedures used for organic analysis include chromatography and mass spectrophotometry. Chromatography is used to separate a sample into its components. The mass spec machine is used to identify the specific constituents within a sample and their relative amounts in the mixture.

. . . .

Concept Reinforcement

1. What is an organic substance?

2. What is chromatography used for in organic analysis?

3. What is the purpose of the mass spectrophotometer machine?

Chapter 29 – Forensic Document Examination

Chapter Objective

- Describe the importance of forensic document examination and how it is used to prove or disprove a crime

Questioned Documents

An object that contains handwriting or print whose authenticity or original source is in question can be considered a **questioned document**. Document examiners have extensive training in order to make a comparison between individual characteristics of questioned documents to either make a match between two samples or reveal a possible forgery. Document examiners may work with a number of different documents and conduct one or more of the following activities:

- Establishment of a forged document from a genuine one

- Detection of erasure marks or substitutions on a document

- Restoration of erased or obliterated writing marks

- Analysis of ink, paper, and chemicals used during the document creation

- Matching handwriting, signatures, or printing to specific individuals

Document examiners may be called upon to match a known and unknown handwriting sample to a specific individual.

Handwriting Analysis

No two individuals have exactly the same handwriting. Differences can be identified between two individual's handwriting samples using the following characteristics: angularity, slope, speed, pressure, letter formation, word spacing, letter dimensions, connections, pen movements, writing skills, and finger dexterity. Handwriting styles arise from habits developed as children learn to write. These writing styles persist into adulthood. Even someone who has a catastrophic injury to their dominant hand will eventually return to the same style preferences as they learn to write with their opposite hand. When a document examiner is called upon to make a comparison between a known and unknown handwriting sample, they must take into account as many of these characteristics as possible. This allows them to establish with a higher degree of certainty if a particular suspect is the potential author of a questioned document. It is very important to secure a collection of as many writing **exemplars** (samples) as possible to make a thorough comparison. A range of exemplars helps the examiner observe a person's natural variations in their writing patterns. No two writing specimens are ever exactly the same when written by the same person because of these natural variations, but the characteristics remain the same. For instance, if you sign your name twice you will notice that the signatures are not identical, but have the same features. Known writing samples should contain the same letters and if possible some of the same words as the questioned document.

Concept Extension: The Lindbergh Kidnapping

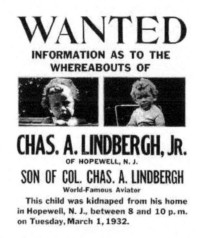

The original ad that ran after the 1932 Charles Lindbergh kidnapping and murder

A famous historical case involving the use of handwriting comparison was the Lindbergh kidnapping of 1932. Charles Lindbergh Jr., the 20-month old son of the wealthy Lindbergh family, was kidnapped from his crib in the evening of March 1, 1932. A ransom note was left that read:

Dear Sir!

Have 50000$ redy 25000$ in
20$ bills 15000$ in 10$ bills and
10000$ in 5$ bills After 2-4 days
we will inform you were to deliver
the Mony.
We warn you for making
anyding public or for notify the Police
The child is in gut care.
Indication for all letters are
singnature
and three holes.

In addition to the letter, a homemade ladder was found outside the toddler's window. The toddler was found dead on May12, 1932 from a severe blow to the head. Several years later, Bruno Hauptmann was arrested and tried for kidnapping and murder. He was convicted and executed by electric chair. A crucial part of the evidence involved handwriting comparisons done between known samples of Hauptmann's writing and the ransom note.

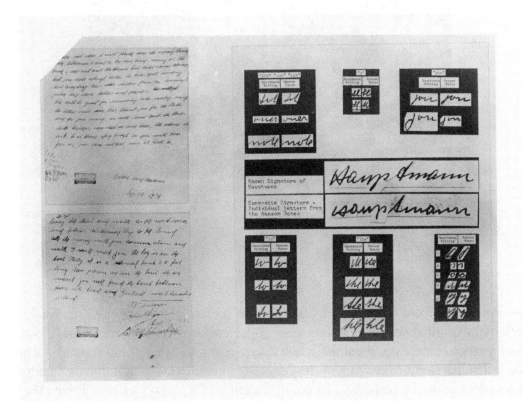

Handwriting samples from Bruno Hauptmann were compared to the ransom note found at the scene.

Printing Devices, Erasures, & Obliterations

In the past, document examination involved the comparison of typeset from notes written using a typewriter. With the advent of digital technology, document examiners now are usually faced with analyzing documents from printers, copiers, or fax machines. Examiners can match a document to a suspected machine by comparing the characteristics left on the paper by a specific machine. Over time a printing device accumulates the characteristics of wear and tear that occur over a random and irregular distribution patterns. Several samples printed on a suspect machine can be compared to the sample in question to make a match. Document examiners also investigate evidence that has been altered through erasures or obliterations. Criminals commonly try to alter documents by erasing certain parts of it. These areas of erasure can be identified using a microscope. Sometimes this content can be recovered utilizing specialized chemicals. A criminal may also attempt to obliterate a document by burning it. Sometimes the charred pieces of a document can be photographed using infrared photography causing a contrast to occur between the writing and charred background. This can be photographed and the digital image enhanced for examination.

Document examiners may be able to recover some
evidence from documents that have been burned.

Summary

A questioned document is an object that contains handwriting or printed material whose authenticity or original source is in question. A professional document examiner is trained for many years to identify and compare individual characteristics of questioned documents to make a comparison or recognize a forgery. Document examiners compare handwriting samples to determine if a suspect is the possible author of a questioned document. They also examine evidence including printer devices, erasures, and obliterations of documents.

Concept Reinforcement

1. What is a questioned document?

2. What characteristics are used when comparing handwriting samples?

3. How is it possible to recover some evidence from documents that have been burned?

Chapter 30 – Voice Print Analysis

Chapter Objective

- Explain the importance of voice print analysis

Voice Evidence

"That voice sounds very familiar" people often say. Every human voice has unique characteristics that can be identified by the human ear. However, this identification is subjective and sometimes two people do sound very similar. The only way to verify that a certain voice belongs to an individual is through **voice print analysis** of a recording. Voice analysis evidence may be admitted into court to verify a recording of a confession or the voice of someone suspected of making a bomb threat.

A voice recording is the only way to verify an individual's voice.

Voice Analysis

In 1963, Lawrence Kersta from the Bell Telephone Laboratories developed a procedure for measuring the pitch, volume, and resonance of a human voice. The voice print of an individual produced by Kersta's device is called a **spectrogram**. The device records a 2.5 second band of speech on a magnetic tape. This tape is then scanned electronically and displayed on a cathode ray tube or printed by a stylus onto a paper feed. Voice spectrograms that are used as evidence in court are typically displayed using a bar print where the horizontal axis represents the recording time length and the vertical axis represents the frequency of the sound being made. The depth of the print illustrates the loudness of the voice. Differences in individual voices are clearly visible on the display, even when two voices sound similar to the human ear.

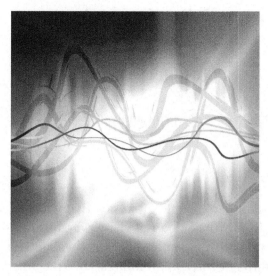

Voice spectrograms provide a visual display of the pitch, frequency, and volume of a human voice.

Case Closed: The Voice Analysis declares it's a hoax

In 1971, Lawrence Kersta was called upon to give his opinion in a case involving voice print evidence. Clifford Irving claimed to have the authorized biography of the famous reclusive millionaire Howard Hughes. He produced letters that he claimed were from Hughes giving him authorization to produce the book. Handwriting experts had certified the letters as genuine. However, after 15 years of reclusion from the public, a man claiming to be Hughes called and in a two-hour phone interview denounced the biography as a complete hoax. Unsure of whether this was actually Hughes on the telephone, the station asked Kersta to compare the voice with a speech that Hughes had given over 30 years earlier. Kersta had near 100% certainty that the voices were a match, thus Irving was arrested and convicted of forgery.

The authorized biography of Howard Hughes (pictured above) that Clifford Irving attempted to publish was declared a forgery using voice print analysis.

Summary

Every human voice has unique characteristics that many times can be identified by the human ear alone. The only method for the verification of a specific individual voice is through recording. Lawrence Kersta of the Bell Telephone Company invented the first device that could record the human voice in the form of a spectrogram. The spectrogram is displayed on a cathode ray screen and demonstrates the frequency and volume of a specific voice. Voice analysis was used in the famous 1971 case involving Clifford Irving. Irving claimed to have the authorized biography of reclusive millionaire Howard Hughes. However, Hughes called from his recluse location to dispute the biography as a forgery. Voice print analysis declared that the voice on the phone was indeed Hughes and Irving was subsequently arrested for forgery.

Concept Reinforcement

1. What is the best method for determining if a voice belongs to a specific individual?

2. What is a spectrogram?

3. How did the authorities determine that Clifford Irving's biography of Howard Hughes was a forgery?

Chapter 31 – Forensic Odontology

Chapter Objective

- Describe forensic dentistry (odontology) and its applications

Forensic Odontology

Forensic odontology is forensic dentistry. Forensic odontology is a branch of forensic medicine that properly examines, handles, and presents dental evidence in a court of law. Forensic odontologists use their skills to help identify unknown corpses using information from the corpse's dentition (teeth). These corpses may be skeletal remains, victims of mass disasters, or murder victims. Forensic odontologists also work with living victims to analyze bite marks and analyze food evidence that has bite marks in it.

Human Dentition

It is important to know that dental enamel is the hardest substance in the human body. This means that teeth are usually the last part of the body to decompose. Human remains at archaeological sites may include teeth from more individuals than the remaining bones would suggest were there. This is because teeth decompose last.

Everyone's teeth are different. The shape and size of our teeth are determined by genetics. Since each person is genetically unique, this means that our teeth are all unique. In addition to basic genetic differences, modern dental practices further differentiate the dental characteristics of each person. Think about your own personal experience. Do you have fillings? Have you lost teeth or had teeth pulled for some reason? Do you have a cap, crown or bridge? Do you have braces? Are your teeth straight or crooked? Do you have a gap between any of your teeth? Are your teeth crowded in your jaw? Each of these dental characteristics makes your mouth more and more unique. The type of bite you have also helps identify you. If you have an overbite, underbite, or cross bite, a forensic odontologist will use it to identify you.

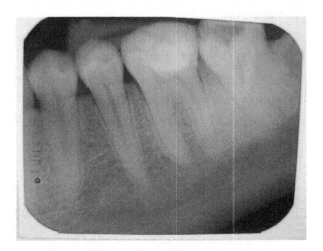

Other factors affect your teeth. These include your age, diet, lifestyle and water source. Your teeth show wear patterns as you age. These patterns depend on what you eat. The food you eat and the things you drink all impact your teeth. For example, if you live in an area with unflouridated water, your teeth will have different characteristics than the teeth of someone who drinks water supplemented with fluoride. Certain drinks stain your teeth, including coffee and red wine.

Your bite, when combined with the shape and size of your teeth, is a powerful tool forensic scientists use to help identify you.

History of Forensic Odontology

Teeth have been used to identify corpses for many years. The Roman Emperor Claudius identified his dead mistress by looking at her teeth. She had a discolored tooth in the front of her mouth. This was in the first century AD, about 2,000 years ago. Paul Revere, who was a dentist, helped identify the Revolutionary War dead by the bridgework in their mouths. It was used to identify Adolph Hitler and Eva Braun after World War II.

Dental evidence was first accepted in the US during the proceedings of the Webster-Parkman case, in which Dr. Nathan Parkman identified the teeth of the murder victim (who had been stabbed, dismembered and burned) by the gold fused to the teeth. This was in 1849. The dental evidence convinced the jury to find Dr. Webster guilty. He was sentenced to death by hanging.

Dr. Oscar Amoedo is considered the father of forensic odontology. He wrote the first book on the topic in 1898, which was titled "L'ArtDentaire en Medicine Legal." Roughly translated, this means Dentistry in Forensic Medicine. 1937 saw the first murder conviction based on bite mark evidence.

Time	Event
~2,000 years ago	The corpse of a beheaded woman was identified based on a discolored tooth.
Revolutionary War	Paul Revere identified war casualties based on their dental bridgework.
World War II	The bodies of Adolph Hitler and Eva Braun were identified based on their dentition.
1849	Dental evidence was first accepted as evidence in a US court during the proceedings of the Webster-Parkman case.
1862	US Armed Forces Institute of Pathology established.
1898	Publication of "L'ArtDentaire en Medicine Legal" by Dr. Oscar Amoedo.
1937	The first murder conviction based on bite mark evidence.
1946	Development of the first system of dental records for use in forensic odontology.

The Tools of Forensic Odontology

Forensic odontologists use a range of tools to help identify individuals. X-rays, dental casts, and photographs are their key tools. These tools are enhanced by databases, imaging tools, and computer graphics tools that assist with modeling teeth and analyzing the evidence.

X-Rays

X-rays are routinely taken as part of dental exams. They help the dentist find problems that are not obvious with a visual exam of the mouth. The image below is a standard dental X-ray. The one beneath that is an orthopantomogram, which is a panoramic X-ray that shows the entire jaw in one image.

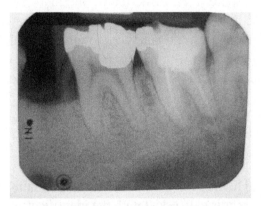

This dental X-ray shows work done on both teeth.

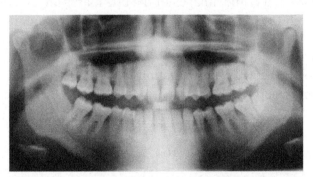

An orthopantomogram (panoramic x-ray) of human teeth.

Forensic odontologists are able to identify individuals based on a comparison of X-rays of the remains and dental X-rays taken during routine dental appointments.

Dental Casts

A dental cast is made by using a tray filled with casting material to get a 3-dimensional copy of the teeth in someone's mouth. The case is then filled with plaster, which is allowed to harden, and creates a model of the teeth as they appear in the jaw. This can be used to compare bite marks to a specific set of teeth, for example. If the cast matches the bite mark, the forensic odontologist is more confident that the person whose teeth were cast actually bit the victim or the piece of food. Remember that everyone's teeth are unique because of age, lifestyle, dental work, and genetics.

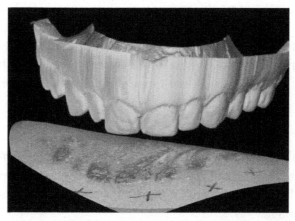

Computer reconstruction of bite mark, 2003
Scientists from the Institute of Forensic Medicine collaborated with police in 2003
to solve a triple homicide. Three women were found beaten to death in an apartment
outside of Zürich, Switzerland. One victim had a bite mark on her shoulder. After
creating dental casts and using 3-D imaging technology to recreate the bite sequence,
scientists were able to prove to a jury that the suspect made the mark. He was found guilty.
Institute of Forensic Medicine, University of Bern

Dental Photography

Dental photography is used to take images of bite marks, remains, and any other situation in which forensic dentists are required to assist with the identification of an individual. Anytime a person is bitten as part of a crime, images of the bite marks are taken and used as evidence in the crime. Because bite marks on living people heal, it is important to take pictures as soon as possible after the bite is made.

The image below is part of an FBI investigation in which bite mark evidence was essential piece of evidence in prosecuting the offender.

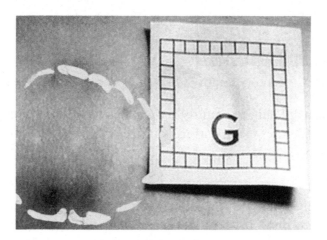

Edges of the defendant's teeth placed next to the corrected image of the bite mark.
The forensic value of this particular comparison is negligible because of the poor
definition of the original injury pattern. The prosecution entered the original
uncorrected bite mark photograph into evidence and argued that a positive dental
identification of the defendant had occurred.

Educational Requirements

What does it take to become a forensic odontologist? In order to become a forensic odontologist, one must have a doctoral degree in dentistry. This may be a DDS, DMD, or equivalent degree. Additional training in forensic dentistry is required. Board certification is also important to prove professional credentials. In the US, the American Board of Forensic Odontology administers the board exam and maintains records of board-certified forensic odontologists.

Summary

Forensic odontology is a branch of forensic medicine that properly examines, handles, and presents dental evidence in a court of law. Since teeth are covered in enamel, which is the most durable substance in the human body, teeth are often the last remnants of a body. Each person also has unique dentition, which is useful in identifying unknown bodies, as well as matching individuals to bitemarks. Forensic odontologists use X-rays, dental casts, and photography as primary tools for analyzing the dental evidence they collect. New technology has improved the ability of the forensic dentist to analyze dental evidence. Forensic odontologists have doctorates in dentistry and typically have board certification to prove their credentials in forensic dentistry.

Concept Reinforcement

1. Describe forensic odontology.

2. Explain how forensic odontologists help identify skeletal remains.

3. Discuss how bite mark evidence is used in criminal investigations.

Chapter 32 – Forensic Anthropology

Chapter Objective

- Describe forensic anthropology and its applications

Forensic Anthropology

Forensic anthropology is a field of forensic science that applies physical anthropology principles and techniques to the legal process. Forensic anthropologists study ancient human remains. These may be fossilized or mummified. These remains provide insight about ancient cultures and the evolution of our species. Forensic anthropologists also study skeletal or badly decomposed human remains in support of criminal investigations. The primary purpose of these studies is to identify the individual. Forensic anthropologists are able to determine age, sex, ancestry, stature, health history and lifestyle of the individual, the age of the skeletal remains, the whether an injury was the cause of death, the time of death and even the number of individuals in a mass grave. Specialists in this field study more than the remains. They also study the environment in which the remains are found. The environment can provide significant clues to the circumstances of death. These include items found in or near the grave site, such as buttons, jewelry, clothing, and anything else that might help identify the individual.

A UN-supported mass grave being excavation in El Mozote, Argentina.
"Image courtesy of the National Institutes of Health

One of the basic roles of the forensic anthropologist is to determine whether the remains are human. Many animal skeletons look like human skeletons. Skeletal bear paws, for example, look like human hands. A forensic anthropologist has the expertise to identify the subtle differences between the bear paw bones and the bones of the human hand.

As with all forensic sciences, forensic anthropologists work with other specialists to determine the overall circumstances of a crime.

History of Forensic Anthropology

Forensic anthropology is a relatively new discipline. Some particularly grisly murders in the 1800s were solved by investigators who studied the remains of the victims. However, anthropology was not officially recognized as important to solving crimes until many years later. The 1930s saw a lot of gangland violence as the various criminal syndicates warred with each other. Forensic anthropologists helped identify the remains of the victims of this war.

The temporary resting place of a Marine killed in the fighting at Lunga Point is shown here. The grave marker was erected by his friends. The Marine's remains were later removed to the division cemetery on Guadalcanal, and further reburial at war's end either in his hometown or the Punchbowl National Cemetery in Hawaii with the honors due a fallen hero.

World War II and the Korean War reinforced the need to identify dead soldiers. Sometimes the soldiers could be identified relatively easily, but other times they could not. If the remains were decomposed or separated from the rest of the body, a forensic anthropologist would help identify the individual. Also, if the remains had decomposed to the point where only skeletal remains were available, the forensic anthropologists were able to use their expertise to determine the basic biological profile of the individual and used that to try to identify an individual. This need to identify the remains of soldiers led to the development of records that would provide clues to the identities of individuals. These health records included age, height, illness history, and dental records. Researchers used this information to develop databases containing statistics on the human skeleton.

Much of forensic anthropology remains focused on bones. New technologies have added to the arsenal of tools available to forensic anthropologists. DNA testing is a powerful tool for identifying individuals. In addition, imaging techniques and extensive databases containing bone statistics are useful in creating the biological profiles that are the basis of forensic anthropology.

Concept Extension: Central Identification Laboratory (CIL)

CIL is the largest forensic anthropology and skeletal identification laboratory in the world. CIL is a unit of the military Joint POW/MIA Accounting Command and located at Hickam Air Force Base, Hawai'i. This laboratory is charged with excavating and identifying the remains of US military and military support personnel.

The three primary objectives of CIL are:

- The recovery and identification of US military personnel, certain American civilian personnel, and certain allied personnel unaccounted for from World War II, the Korean War, the Vietnam War, and other conflicts and contingencies.

- To serve as a national forensic resource.

- To advance research and development in the area of forensic science as it relates to the recovery and identification of human remains.

CIL teams are deployed to various places around the world where American remains have been discovered. Some of the key areas are Europe and Southeast Asia, which makes sense based on the locations of 20th century wars and military conflicts. Teams are deployed to sites on mountainsides, in jungles, under water and other remote, challenging sites. The team has to go to the site, so they must be prepared to work in adverse conditions for long periods of time. A mission usually lasts 30-60 days.

MICRONESIA (Feb. 14, 2008) Petty Officer 1st Class Julius Mcmanus, assigned to Mobile Diving Salvage Unit (MDSU) 1, plants an American flag on the site where an American WWII military aircraft crashed into the Pacific Ocean. Deep sea divers are assigned to Joint POW/MIA Accounting Command (JPAC) accounting of all Americans missing as a result of the nation's past conflicts. Image courtesy of: United States Navy, Mass Communication Specialist 2nd Class Christopher Perez

Forensic anthropologists lead the excavation and recovery activities of the teams. They follow precise protocols to document the site, excavate the remains, and protect and transport the remains. Once the remains are at the CIL, they are signed over to an evidence technician, who is then responsible for maintaining the chain of custody.

On average, CIL identifies the remains of about six MIAs each month, bringing closure to their families. So far, the US Government has identified over 1,300 individuals.

CIL has other functions:

- Conduct research on forensic science methods and techniques

- Support humanitarian missions in supports of homeland defense, current day mishaps, and national and international mass disasters

- Provide forensic support to foreign governments and international organizations.

- Provide forensic support to law enforcement and investigative agencies.

- Collaborate with national and international scientific and forensic organization to advance the field.

The Tools of Forensic Anthropology

Some people may joke that the primary tool of a forensic anthropologist is a shovel, but this is not true. Forensic anthropology often requires the excavation of a grave site, which requires shovels, but the technical tools used by the forensic anthropologists are more important to identifying the individual.

> Ante-mortem
>
> Before (Ante) death (mortem)

The primary tool of the forensic anthropologist is the biological profile. A biological profile is a reconstruction of the person's life and death, including biological sex, chronological age, ante-mortem trauma, ancestry and stature. Forensic anthropologists use their training and extensive databases containing bone characteristics to build the biological profile. The biological profile helps narrow the potential matches to the individual represented by the remains.

Biological age can be determined based on well-defined characteristics of bones at different stages of development. The bones of children and young adults have different fundamental traits than those of adults. The long bones of the body (those found in the arms and legs) grow from ossification centers, which coalesce (join) to form the diaphyses (shafts) and epiphyses (ends) of the long bones. These parts of the bone continue to grow as the person's body develops to adulthood. At a certain age, they begin to fuse together, which stops the growth of the shaft. This process is calledepiphyseal union. Epiphyseal union occurs at different ages, based on sex and ancestry.

The bones tell the forensic anthropologist about any injuries sustained by the individual, and may provide clues regarding the cause of death. For example, a fractured skull might be the cause of death. The shape of the fracture may also provide clues about how the fracture occurred. Was it the result of an accidental fall? Was it the result of a baseball bat connecting with the person's head?

Another important tool in forensic anthropology is DNA analysis. If the anthropologist tentatively identifies an individual, it is sometimes possible to confirm this identification using DNA from a related individual. This is not always possible because sometimes the remains are so old or degraded that the DNA is either not available or so damaged that it is not possible to do a good comparison. The mitochondrial DNA is the most useful in identifying skeletal remains. This is because mtDNA can be extracted from bony tissue. Mitochondrial DNA (mtDNA) is DNA from the mother (or maternal line), so can be used to identify siblings and children that are biologically related to the individual's mother. If the individual is male, mtDNA from a sister or mother can be used for this purpose. If the individual is female, investigators can also compare the mtDNA with mtDNA from her children.

Long Bone

- Epiphysis
- Articular cartilage
- Ephiphyseal line
- Spongy bone
- Medullary cavity
- Nutrient foramen
- Diaphysis
- Endosteum
- Periosteum
- Articular cartilage
- Epiphysis

A computer-generated image of a skull fracture

Diaphyses
Bone shafts

Epiphyses
End of a bone, where the joint occurs.

Epiphyseal Union
The process of fusion between the diaphyses and epiphyses that stops the growth of the shaft of the bone.

Educational Requirements

A forensic anthropologist must go through extensive education. The first step is a bachelor's degree in chemistry, biology, anatomy, physiology or anthropology. This takes about four years. The second step is to pursue a graduate degree, most likely a doctorate, in anthropology or human biology. This takes at least another 3 years, but could take longer. In addition to the doctorate (Ph.D.), three years of field experience are required if you want to seek board certification. Most forensic anthropologists work at universities, teaching students and conducting research. They also consult with medical examiners and the court system. A few work for the military and conduct remains recovery missions to find missing American military personnel.

Summary

Forensic anthropology is a field of forensic sciences that applies physical anthropology principles and techniques to the legal process. A forensic anthropologist creates a biological profile to define specific characteristics of the individual. The biological profiles include stature, chronological age, biological sex, ancestry, and ante-mortem trauma. DNA, particularly mitochondrial DNA, can be used to match an individual with living relatives. The key is that mtDNA comes from the maternal line, so must come from a person that is related through the mother. Forensic Anthropologists must go through extensive education and training before they can obtain board certification. A PhD plus board certification is the most attractive set of credentials for a forensic anthropologist.

Concept Reinforcement

1. Describe forensic anthropology.

2. Explain how forensic anthropologists help identify skeletal remains.

3. List the key parts of a biological profile and state why these characteristics are important in identifying individuals from skeletal remains.

Chapter 33 – Forensic Entomology

Chapter Objective

- Describe forensic entomology and its applications

Forensic Entomology

Forensic entomology uses the knowledge of insect life cycles and habitats to determine the approximate time of death and whether the body was moved from one location to another. Forensic entomologists specialize in flies and other insects that feed on corpses. These insects include flies, beetles, mites, isopods, opiliones, and nematodes. The insects feed, breed, and/or live on or in the corpse. This depends on the preferences of the insects and the state of decomposition of the corpse. Forensic entomologists are used in cases that involve both human and non-human bodies. Cases of poaching, which is illegal hunting, sometimes benefit from the expertise of a forensic entomologist.

Insects tend to show up at a corpse in a predictable pattern. This pattern varies from place to place, but is consistent for a specific location. Geographic region, locale, time of day and season all affect the behavioral and developmental patterns of insects. In addition, some insects are there to feed on the corpse, while others are there to eat the first insects that showed up.

History of Forensic Entomology

The first documented entomology case is from 13th century China. Sung Tz'u was a Chinese lawyer, death investigator and the author of a medical-legal text titled "Hsi Yuan Lu." This title roughly translates to the washing away of wrongs. The case involved a stabbing that occurred near a rice field. The investigator solved the crime by making the workers lay down their sickles (sharp bladed agricultural tools) and watching which tool attracted the blow flies. The owner of the tool confessed when confronted with the evidence.

Artists, sculptors, painters and poets have also contributed to our knowledge of insect behavior through their observations of body decomposition. These artists sometimes depicted the insects feeding on corpses.

The role of insects in forensic investigations was further established in Germany and France during the late 1880s when Reinhard and Hofmann were performing mass exhumations. Mégnin published a book on applied forensic entomology, which helped the idea of entomology as a forensic investigation tool spread quickly to North America. This led to the development of extensive information on insect life cycles and behavior related to corpses.

Some of the first case reports that relied on forensic entomology were related to child deaths that were suspected to have involved sulphuric acid. Scientists proved that ants, cockroaches and freshwater arthropods caused the damage to the corpses after death. The abrasions on the corpses were the result of the feeding behavior of the insects and not child abuse.

Interest in the impact of insects on the decomposition of bodies continued through the world wars, with scientists developing extensive information on the insects that feed on corpses, as well as the order in which they appear on a corpse, their life cycles and behavioral patterns. Research has continued and forensic entomology is now a standard tool used to investigate murders and other cases involving decomposing bodies.

Concept Extension: Blow Flies

Blowflies are usually the first insects to show up at a corpse. The lay their eggs in the moist areas of the corpse, such as the nose, mouth, armpit, groin, and open wounds. It only takes 24 hours for the eggs to hatch. Larvae (also known as maggots) feed and grow on the corpse. The larvae molt several times over the next 10 days or so. At this point, they become pupae, which means that their outer covering hardens. The pupae continue to develop for the next 12 days, when adult flies emerge from the shell, starting the cycle all over.

A blow fly, Calliphora sp. (Diptera: Calliphoridae), on a red tulip.
Morrisburg, Ontario, Canada.
Image courtesy of Sue Welsh

The Tools of Forensic Entomology

The tools of forensic entomology are those required to understand the insects. The basic tools include nets, vials, fly traps, pencils, cameras, thermometers, forceps, labels, and rulers. These tools are used to capture and document the insects found on the body while they are still on the body, and to then capture the insects for further laboratory analysis.

The extensive databases containing insect life cycles and their interaction with decomposing flesh. The insects found on decomposing corpses are also able to provide information on whether the victim was poisoned. This field, called entomotoxicology, uses the insects to test for specific toxins, or poisons, that might have contributed to the victim's death.

Some of the techniques used by forensic entomologists include scanning electron microscopy, potassium permanganate staining, and gene expression,

Scanning Electron Microscopy is used to identify specific species of fly eggs found on a corpse, especially when the corpse is very fresh. It is difficult to identify specific species of blow fly eggs with the naked eye or a standard microscope. The SEM allows investigators to get a clear, high magnification image to help them identify the species of fly. The SEM allows forensic entomologists to see small morphological differences between the eggs, which allow them to identify the species of fly. This technique is not useful in the field, but can be useful in cases where there is time to move the eggs to a laboratory with a scanning electron microscope.

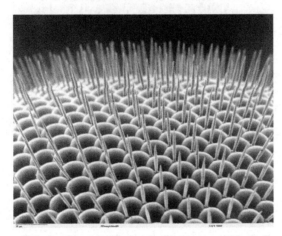

Scanning electron microscope image of an eye on a fruit fly. Image is a high magnification view of part of the eye. Class Insecta; Order Diptera – flies; Super Family Drosophiloidea; Family Drosophilidae- fruit fly
Image courtesy of Dartmouth College

Potassium permanganate staining is another technique that can be used to identify fly species from their eggs. Potassium permanganate is a commonly used laboratory stain that helps show the characteristics of the sample more clearly. The eggs are soaked in saline solution and moved to a glass petri dish, where they are then soaked in a 1% potassium permanganate solution for 1 minute. The eggs are then dehydrated and analyzed under a light microscope. The staining allows the investigator to better see the characteristics of the eggs to help determine the insect species.

Gene expression is the study of which genes are active and inactive during certain stages of development or disease. When genes are expressed (upregulated or turned on), they actively produce proteins that serve specific purposes in the body. When they are downregulated (not expressed or turned off), they do not produce proteins. This is a useful tool in understanding the developmental stage of insects. The developmental stage is then used to determine the post-mortem interval, which is the time since death.

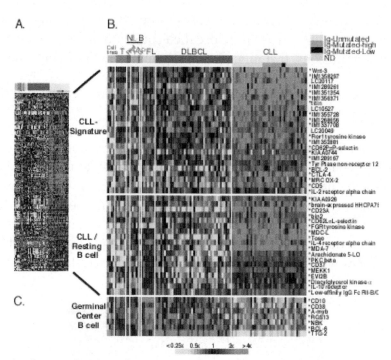

This image is the result of a microarray experiment, which shows gene expression. The green areas show where genes are active (being expressed/upregulated). The red areas show the inactive genes, which are those that are not being expressed and are downregulated. Image courtesy of the National Institutes of Health

Educational Requirements

A forensic entomologist must complete extensive education. A person interested in working in this field will usually pursue an undergraduate degree in entomology, the study of insects. It is also possible to pursue an undergraduate degree in forensic science with an emphasis in entomology. In order to teach forensic entomology or be considered a professional forensic entomologist, it is important to obtain a graduate degree, either at the masters or doctoral level. These degrees are in entomology or a related field, with a focus on forensic entomology. The American Board of Forensic Entomology offers a board certification exam to those with at least a masters of science degree.

Summary

Forensic entomology is focused on using entomological knowledge in support of medical-legal cases. Forensic entomology is used in a variety of cases, including cases that have human or non-human remains. Forensic entomology has been studied for a long time, but became organized as a scientific discipline starting in the 1800s. Investigators began to study the life cycles and behavior of insects as it relates to decomposing flesh. They learned that insects follow very specific patterns relative to the decomposition of a body. Some show up immediately after death, like the blow fly. Others come to the body to feed on the insects feeding on the body. The patterns vary by time of day, location, weather, and other variables. These patterns are well documents, so forensic entomologists have substantial resources available to them to determine the post-mortem interval (PMI), which is the time since death. Forensic entomologists use basic tools, such as vials, fly catchers, and cameras, to do basic documentation and capture samples of insects. They also benefit from more advanced technologist, such as scanning electron microscopes and gene expression, to further refine their analyses. A professional forensic entomologist typically has a masters or doctoral degree and may have achieved board certification.

Concept Reinforcement

1. Describe forensic entomology.

2. Explain how forensic entomologists help establish time of death.

3. Explain how SEM and gene expression help refine the analysis done by a forensic entomologist.

Chapter 34 – Forensic Psychiatry

Chapter Objective

- Describe forensic psychiatry and its applications

Forensic Psychiatry

Forensic psychiatry is a branch of psychiatry that is adversarial rather than therapeutic. Forensic psychiatry works to dissect the personality and motives of the accused. As a result, the forensic psychiatrist must have extensive knowledge of human behavior, both normal and abnormal, and be able to determine whether the accused is lying or trying to be deceitful. In some cases, the accused will try to fabricate an insanity defense by behaving strangely or exaggerating particular aspects of their personality related to the crime.

Here is a list of potential uses of forensic psychiatry:

- Assess the role of drugs or alcohol in the crime

- Determine sanity or competency to stand trial

- Assess a subject's grasp of reality and responsibility

- Offer judgment on the individual's state of mind at the time of the crime.

- Provide information to investigators for use in witness and suspect interrogations.

- Create a psychological profile of the type of criminal who probably committed the crime

- Determine competency for signing legal documents, managing personal affairs, voting, to care for self or others, to offer testimony, or to stand trial.

- Perform a psychological autopsy in cases of suicide.

Forensic psychiatry is used in a variety of cases, including violent crimes. It is also used in personal injury cases where an individual claims to have been harmed psychologically by an incident, whether it is an accident, abuse, or something else. Forensic psychiatry is also used to determine mental competence. This is often necessary in cases involving the elderly. Sometimes people lose their capacity to function and care for themselves. In these cases, a forensic psychiatrist will assess the person's competence in terms of evaluating and making decisions and capacity, and report his findings to the court. If the person is found incompetent, the court may put the elderly person in the care of an individual or an institution that is able to provide the necessary support.

A forensic psychiatric evaluation will generally include the following:

- Complete medical history

- Psychiatric medical status examination

- Psychological assessment

- Review of pertinent medical records, discovery and evidentiary deposition transcripts, school records, work product, and any related materials.

- The results of neuropsychological tests

- A forensic brain injury evaluation is done in cases where brain injury is obvious or suspected. The brain injury may be a result of trauma, loss of oxygen (hypoxia), stroke (ischemia), or toxins/chemicals. The evaluations will generally include the following:

- Neurological Exam

- Neuropsychological assessment

- Structural and/or functional brain images

- Lab studies

History of Forensic Psychiatry

Forensic psychiatry has a fascinating history. People as far back as 180 AD were aware that some might simulate insanity. Macer, who wrote about the time of Marcus Aurelius, attempted to define insanity with the following statement he gave as an expert witness in the trial of a man who killed his mother.

"If you have clearly ascertained that the defendant is in such a state of insanity that he is permanently out of his mind and so entirely incapable of reasons, and no suspicion is left behind that he was simulating insanity when he killed his mother, you need not concern yourself with the question how he should be punished...he should be kept on close observations, and, if you think it advisable, even kept in restraint..."

Read the statement carefully. This statement recognizes that the defendant, if truly insane, should not be held responsible for his actions. He should, instead, be institutionalized and observed, in restraints, if necessary. Under Aurelius, the family was often held responsible for the actions of an insane family member, up to and including execution of a sane family member in response to the actions of the insane one.

African societies used truth pellets to determine guilt or innocence. They lined up the suspects of a serious crime and placed truth pellets in their mouths. They told the suspects that the pellet would poison the guilty person, but not harm the innocent. They really used small scraps of leather and took advantage of a physiological fear response – dry mouth. The suspects whose "truth pellets" were wet when removed from their mouths were considered innocent. The guilty person would not have enough saliva to moisten the leather, which is how the determination of guilt was made.

Many early cultures differentiated between intentional and unintentional homicide, setting different penalties depending upon whether the crime was intentional or not. Others, especially in medieval Europe, believed that mentally ill people had sold their souls to the devil, which justified executions, including witch executions, to protect the rest of the population.

European countries later used a more "medical" approach to diagnosing mental illness. Physicians used diagnoses such as ruled by humors, delirious, affected by mania, and monomania as diagnoses for mental illness. These diagnoses carried a lot of negative connotations, so people with these diagnoses were stigmatized.

Immanuel Kant was a philosopher who tried to separate the diagnoses relevant to forensic psychiatry into four groups: amentia, dementia, insania, and vesania. Amentia was defined as chaotic thought; dementia as delusions of reference and an inability to separate reality from fantasy; insania as disturbed judgment or flight of ideas; and vesania as disorder of reason. Psychiatric testimony became part of the trial process in the 19th century when independent medical witnesses began to provide expert medical testimony on psychiatric issues.

Concept Extension: The Psychopath

Early on, psychopaths were describe as being morally insane, which implies a psychiatric problem, but not necessarily a cognitive problem. A psychopath is able to think clearly, but does not have the moral compass required to keep their behavior within societal norms. A psychopath may be extremely charming, but totally devoid of empathy, guilt or love. They are self-centered, dishonest and undependable. They engage in irresponsible behavior just for the fun of it and are unable to have truly intimate romantic relationships. Psychopaths often refuse to take responsibility for their actions, sometimes blaming others or making excuses. They have difficulty restraining themselves from their bad behavior and do not learn from their mistakes or from negative feedback.

Misperception	Reality
All psychopaths are violent	Most psychopaths are not violent. Most violent people are NOT psychopaths. Psychopathy is a risk factor for future violence.
All psychopaths are psychotic	Psychopaths are almost always rational. Psychotic disorders involve losing touch with reality, which is not a sign of rationality.
Psychopathy is untreatable	The criminal behaviors of psychopaths may be amenable to treatment even if the core psychopathic personality traits are difficult to change.

Psychopathy is measured using the Psychopathy Checklist-Revised (PCL-R), which was developed by Robert D. Hare. This assessment includes a standardized interview with the subject and an examination of criminal, medical and educational histories. Analyses of the results of this instrument have shown three sets of traits of a psychopath.

- Interpersonal deficits (for example, grandiosity, arrogance, deceitfulness)

- Affective deficits (for example, lack of guilt, lack of empathy)

- Impulsive and criminal behaviors (for example, sexual promiscuity and stealing)

The Tools of Forensic Psychiatry

Psychiatry is a field of medicine related to the psyche, or mental state, of an individual. Many standard assessment tools have been developed to establish the risk of violent behavior. These tools are not completely accurate, but to provide a good prediction of behavior.

One type of assessment tool is called an actuarial instrument. The actuarial instrument attached specific statistical weights to individual variables. The weighting schemes used in these instruments are based on observations of similar individuals over time. In theory, these tools will help predict the likelihood of violent behavior in a group. Examples of actuarial instruments are the VRAG (Violent Risk Appraisal Guide); SORAG (Sex Offender Risk Appraisal Guide); Psychopathy Checklist-Revised; and the Violence Risk Assessment Scale (VRS). There are many others.

Structured clinical guides, however, are used by clinicians to assess the risk of future violence by an individual. These guides allow psychiatrists to use a quantitative (number-based) approach to assessment. The guides include the Spousal Assault Risk Assessment Guide (SARA), Sexual Violence Risk-20 (SVR-20), Structured Assessment of Violence Risk in Youth (SAVRY), and the Workplace Risk Assessment (WRA-20). As with actuarial instruments, there are many other structured clinical guides available to forensic psychiatrists.

Forensic psychiatrists also have modern technology available to them. Scientists have been conducting research on the physiology of the brain using sophisticated imaging techniques and biological marker tests. These tests are not yet readily accepted as evidence in a trial for a number of reasons. There are a number of different brain imaging technologies that show different characteristics of the brain and its functions. These include:

- computed tomography (CT)

- magnetic resonance imaging (MRI)

- functional magnetic resonance imaging (fMRI)

- blood oxygenation level-dependent (BOLD) fMRI

- diffusion tensor imaging (TSI)

- magnetic resonance spectroscopy (MRS)

- quantitative electroencephalography (qEEG)

- positron emission tomography (PET)

- single-photon emission computed tomography (SPECT)

- magnetoencephalography (MEG)

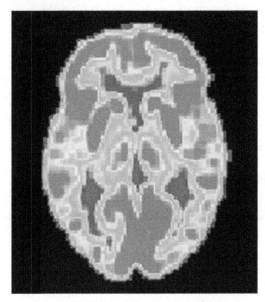

A PET Scan of a human brain

Each of these techniques produces a detectable signal that indicates a specific measure of brain activity. These signals must be interpreted using a model, which is based on a set of assumptions. The resulting reconstruction allows clinicians to draw inferences, but not definitive statements, about a patient. The steps involved with brain imaging are not standardized and are easily manipulated by someone with the appropriate technical expertise.

Another reason these imaging techniques are not yet ready for standard use as evidence is that the definition of "normal" is elusive. Normal may mean the exclusion of physiological disease. It may also mean the exclusion of psychological disease. It is not yet clear what "normal" is in terms of the human brain. It is also not clear where the abnormal actually becomes the dysfunctional, either physically or psychiatrically.

Educational Requirements

A psychiatrist is a medical doctor who has received additional training in the understanding, diagnosis and treatment of mental disorders. A forensic psychiatrist has even more training and/or experience in applying the techniques of psychiatry to legal issues.

Summary

Forensic psychiatry is important in assessing the mental state of victims or the accused in cases of the law. It is also used in civil courts to determine competency to care for oneself or others, manage personal affairs, offer testimony, etc. The primary tools of the forensic psychiatrist are assessment tools, the results of which are based on interviews of the subject. Certain lab tests can be used in conjunction with forensic psychiatry, including those that show exposure to different drugs, but brain imaging is not yet a standard tool in the arsenal of the forensic psychiatrist. A forensic psychiatrist has a medical degree with the additional training to understand, diagnosis and treat mental disorders as well as in applying the techniques of psychiatry to legal issues.

. . . .

Concept Reinforcement

1. Describe forensic psychiatry.

2. Explain how forensic psychiatrists assess mental state.

3. Explain why brain imaging techniques are not yet readily accepted as evidence by the courts.

Chapter 35 – Forensic Profiling

Chapter Objective

- Describe forensic profiling and its applications

Forensic Profiling

Forensic profiling is the process of looking at evidence and making a best guess about the type of individual who would commit the crime. A profiler usually has specific training, often from the FBI (in the US). The profiler examines the crime scene, victim, autopsy data and likely pre-crime and post-crime behaviors of the killer to develop a profile. Once of the basic concepts of profiling is that behavior reflects personality.

A criminal leaves several types of evidence at a crime scene: physical, behavioral and psychiatric. The forensic profiler uses all of these to develop a picture of the offender. The resulting profile is used by investigators to narrow down the search for the criminal and hopefully make an arrest.

The crime scene will also contain evidence of the criminal's MO and signature, which are two different things.

The **MO (Modus operandi, or method of operation)** includes the tools and strategies used by the criminal. These tools and strategies are all designed to help the criminal get away with the crime. MOs will evolve over time as the criminal gains experience.

The **signature**, on the other hand, is an act that has nothing to do with committing or getting away with the crime. Signatures may include taking trophies, torture, overkills, and postmortem posing or mutilation. Signatures are the result of the psychological needs and fantasies of the offender. Signatures stay the same. They do NOT evolve.

The profiler goes through a process of asking questions and obtaining answers, such as the following:

- How did the criminal gain access to the crime scene or the victim?

- What did the criminal do?

- Did the criminal try to hide his tracks?

- Why was the victim or crime scene attractive to the criminal?

- What was the criminal's motive?

The profile of a serial murderer provides information on the physical and psychological makeup of the offender, where the offenders has lived or worked, possible pre-crime behaviors, and post-crime movements.

> Atcherley's 10 point system for identifying a criminal's MO
>
> Location of the crime
>
> Point of entry
>
> Method of entry
>
> Tools used
>
> Types of objects taken
>
> Time of day the crime was committed
>
> Alibi
>
> Accomplices
>
> Method of transportation
>
> Unusual features of the crime

History of Forensic Profiling

Criminal profiling goes back to the early 1800s. A number of investigators, such as Jacob Fries and Hans Gross, made small contributions to early forensic profiling, but are not considered part of the field of criminal profiling.

The first case of modern profiling was related to the Jack the Ripper case in London in the 1890s. Dr. Thomas bond performed an autopsy on Jack the Ripper's last victim, Mary Kelly, and learned that the killer did not understand anatomy. He reconstructed the murder in an attempt to understand the events of the assault and tried to interpret the behavior of killer. He developed a profile, which he provided to the police. The profile included a quiet, harmless looking man who was strong physically, composed, daring, a loner and without an occupation. He also concluded that all five murders attributed to Jack the Ripper were committed by the same man. The case was never solved, but Dr. Bond's work helped launch the field of offender profiling.

Adolph Hitler was the next major subject of criminal profiling. In 1943, Dr. Walter Langer was asked by the US Office of Strategic Services to profile Hitler. Langer studies Hitler's speeches and writings and interviewed people who knew Hitler. The profile he developed described Hitler as meticulous, conventional, prudish about his appearance and body, healthy physically and deteriorating mentally. He noted that Hitler constantly had to prove his masculinity to his mother and predicted that Hitler would probably commit suicide if he was defeated. Hitler did, in fact, commit suicide.

A major case in the use involved the Mad Bomber of New York in 1956. Dr. James Brussellswas asked by the NYPD to develop a profile on the bomber. Again, Brussell studied crime scene photographs and the bomber's letters to the press to better understand the bomber. Brussell's profile describe the bomber as a middle-aged, heavy man who was foreign born, Roman Catholic, single and living with a sibling. He also predicted the bomber's clothing – a double breasted suit that he would wear buttoned. Brussell was accurate all the way down to the details of the clothing.

Concept Extension: Types of offenders

There are three main categories of offenders: organized, disorganized, and mixed.

Organized offenders are sophisticated in their approach to crime. They often have high intelligence and plan their crimes carefully. They are usually employed and may have families and long-term social relationships. Organized offenders are controlled despite their fantasies, and are able to mask their criminal tendencies until they are ready to commit the crime. The planning consists of preparation and rehearsal, targeting the victim, determining the techniques they will use to control the victim, select the tools they will use, and, if they are going to kill the victim, a place to hide or bury the body.

Disorganized offenders tend to be loners and have lower than average intelligence. They may be unemployed or work at low-paying jobs. Mental illness is often present. Disorganized offenders do not have control – they act impulsively and do not plan their crimes. They are unable to control their fantasies and act on them. Attacks are not subtle, as they are with the organized offenders. Disorganized offenders tend to attack suddenly, violently and viciously, overwhelming the victim. This results in a messy crime scene. Because disorganized offenders do not plan ahead, they do not bring tools with them. As a result, they use whatever is handy when they can no longer resist the urge to strike. If they kill, they usually leave the body behind. The do not try to cover up the evidence that they were there.

Mixed offenders show characteristics of both organized and disorganized offenders. They may plan their crimes and have a MO, but not follow through to ensure that there is no evidence of their presence. The assault may be very messy or frenzied, leaving a large amount of evidence at the scene. This may indicate that the mixed offender has some control over his or her violent fantasies, but is unable to completely control them.

The Tools of Forensic Profiling

Forensic profilers profile both criminals and victims. The primary tool of a profiler, besides her extensive knowledge of human behavior, is a set of descriptors that used to describe the types of individuals who commit crimes or who tend to be victims of crime.

The descriptors include age, sex, race, residency, proximity, social skills, work and military histories, and educational level.

The FBI uses two processes for developing criminal profiles: Crime scene analysis and behavioral evidence analysis. We will look at them one at a time.

Crime scene analysis is a 6-step procedure followed by the FBI. The steps are profiling inputs, decision process models, crime assessment, criminal profile, investigation and apprehension.

Step	Description
Profiling Inputs	A collection of all the evidence from the crime, including physical evidence from the scene, victims or the accused, as well as any documentation from the crime scene, including notes, sketches, and photographs.
Decision Process Models	The evidence is arranged and examined for any patterns. These patterns can include location, similarities between the victims, similarities in the commission of the crime, etc.
Crime Assessment	The crime scene is reconstructed, using patterns to determine when each event happened, the order of events, and who did what.
Criminal Profile	The first three steps are used to develop a criminal profile. The profile also includes the physical qualities, motives and personality of the perpetrator. This information is used to determine the style of interview used when interrogating the accused.
Investigation	Once the profile is developed, it is provided to the criminal investigators responsible for the case. It is also distributed to organizations that may be able to help identify the suspect. If no leads are developed or new information is found, the profile will probably be reassessed and refined.

Apprehension (the arrest)	Investigators are able to arrest a suspect about half the time. If, after the interview, investigation, comparison to the profile, etc., the investigator is convinced the suspect is the perpetrator, an arrest warrant is obtained. This is followed by a trial, unless a deal is made or something happens to damage the case so it cannot go to trial.

The second process used to develop a criminal profile is **behavioral evidence analysis**. This tool was created by Brent Turvey because he felt the most objective record of a criminal event is a reconstruction of offender behavior. This process has four steps: equivocal forensic analysis, victimology, crime scene characteristics, and offender characteristics.

Step	Description
Equivocal Forensic Analysis	Analysis of the physical evidence. This includes the physical evidence of the crime, interview records, evidence logs, investigator and autopsy reports, photographs, videos, autopsy, and living victims.
Victimology	In this step, the investigator creates a profile of the victim, including physical, psychological, and lifestyle parameters. Victims tend to fall into three categories: high, medium and low risk. Offenders often select their victims based on specific characteristics.
Crime Scene Characteristics	This is an analysis of the crime scene, including location relative to the world, the location where the majority of the crime occurred, as well as the position of the body, the state or oganization or disorganization of the scene, etc.
Offender Characteristics	The first three steps are used to develop a rough character sketch.

CODIS

Combined DNA Index System, a database of DNA profiles used by law enforcement agencies.

The profiles are often submitted to CODIS, an FBI database that contains information on crimes and criminals for use by the law enforcement community. The profiles developed by the forensic profiler may match characteristics of a case in CODIS, which helps narrow the search for the perpetrator.

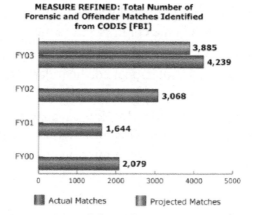

Image courtesy of the US Department of Justice

186

Educational Requirements

Criminal profiling is not a common job in the law enforcement community. There are, therefore, few programs dedicated to criminal profiling and forensic psychology. A forensic psychologist usually earns a degree in clinical, developmental, social or cognitive psychology, which they then follow with specialized coursework in criminal justices and law. You are more likely to learn how to be a profiler by pursuing a law enforcement degree and working in the field. The FBI, for example, requires special agents who do profiling tasks for the National Center for the Analysis of Violent Crime to have at least three years of experience as a special agent for the FBI before they are considered for assignment to NCAVC.

> NCAVC
>
> National Center for the Analysis of Violent Crime

Summary

Forensic profiling is a highly specialized field in law enforcement. Agencies do not often hire people specifically to profile cases, criminals and victims, but they do have people who are specially trained to develop profiles. A criminal profile incorporates information in the criminal (age, sex, personality type, etc), as well as information about the crime scene and a profile of the victim. These pieces of information are used to develop an overall picture of the crime. The primary tool of a forensic profiler is the set of descriptors used to define individuals, as well as her extensive knowledge of human behavior.

....

Concept Reinforcement

1. Describe forensic profiling.

2. Explain how forensic profilers reconstruct a crime scene.

3. State the two tools used by the FBI to develop criminal profiles and list the steps of each tool.

Chapter 36 – Forensic Interviewing

Chapter Objective

- Describe forensic interviewing and its applications

Forensic Interviewing

Forensic interviewing is used when questioning the alleged victims of child abuse or adult sexual abuse. Forensic interviewing is different than interrogation, which is used by the police when questioning suspected criminals.

The primary purpose of a forensic interview is to find out if the victim was, in fact, mistreated. The key secondary purpose of the forensic interview is to collect evidence that will stand up in court. In order for the evidence to be acceptable during a trial, the evidence must be collected in an objective, consistent and carefully documented manner.

The primary goals of a forensic interview are:

- Maximize Information

- Increase Accuracy

- Legally Defensible

- Developmentally Sensitive

- Minimize Impact to Victim

Forensic interviewers work to collect as much information as possible from the interview subject. It is important that the interview gather as much accurate information as the interviewee is able to give. In order for the content of the interview to be admissible in court, the interviewer must follow the strict protocols required for gathering evidence used in the courtroom. The forensic interviewer must be sensitive to the developmental level of the person being interviewed. Children are at a different developmental stage than adults, therefore need to be interviewed differently to ensure the maximum information is gathered during the interview while minimizing any further trauma to the alleged victim of the crime.

Forensic interviews are similar to social work interviews, but much more focused and used during the assessment portion of an investigation into the abuse of a child or adult. The forensic interview is used only with the alleged victim, not the perpetrator. The techniques for interviewing victims and perpetrators are very different. Victim interviews are non-threatening. Interviews with alleged perpetrators are more likely to be confrontational.

> The Three Requirements for a Forensic Interview to Stand up in Court
>
> Interviewer objectivity
>
> Use of non-leading questions and interview techniques
>
> Careful documentation of the interview.

History of Forensic Psychology

Forensic interviewing is a component of forensic psychology. A significant development in forensic psychology was the establishment of a psychology laboratory by Wilhelm Wundt in 1879.

The Wilhelm Wundt Research Group

Wundt was instrumental in developing the experimental method in terms of psychology studies. The experimental method provides a rigid framework for applied psychological investigations. A research study using this technique was conducted in 1895. The researcher conducted experiments on the nature of testimony. His findings highlighted the effects of situational and individual differences in how testimony is given. Hugo Munsterberg was an experimental psychologist who studied under Wilhelm Wundt in Leipzig. Munsterberg move to the US in 1892 and established an experimental laboratory at Harvard. His goal was to introduce applied psychology to the courtroom. While the legal system did not accept Munsterberg's ideas, he continued to do research and promote forensic psychology. He conducted research into witness memory, false confessions, and hypnosis, particularly as it could be used in legal proceedings.

Concept Extension: Police Interrogation

Police interrogations are very different than forensic interviews. A police interrogation is a confrontational exchange in which there is some presumption of guilt on the part of the person being questioned. The interrogation exploits weaknesses in human nature. People experience stress when they are subjected to extremes, such as dominance and submission; control and dependence; and the maximization and minimization of consequences. Police interrogation techniques take advantage of these stress responses to gain information and confessions to crimes.

Historically, police investigations could be very coercive, often resulting in false confessions. This issue was finally taken to the Supreme Court of the US in the case of Miranda v. Arizona. In this situation, the Ernesto Miranda confessed to a rape and kidnapping that he did not do. He made this confession after two hours of interrogation. The Supreme Court ruled in Miranda's favor and the Miranda Warning was enacted in 1966. The goal was to reduce coercive police interrogations resulting in false confessions by ensuring that all suspects were given the Miranda Warning. This warning outlines the suspect's rights, including the right to counsel (a lawyer – 6th Amendment) and the right to remain silent (the 5th Amendment). The Miranda warning must be given when a person is being arrested. If it is not given, any confessions or other evidence gained by the police are not admissible in court.

Once Miranda went into effect, police tried other interrogation tools. These include good cop/bad cop, in which one interrogator is very aggressive and threatening with the suspect, while the other acts nicer and tries to gain the confidence of the suspect in hopes that the suspect will talk more. Maximization is another technique used to intimidate suspects. The interrogator will tell the suspect all the awful things that might happen to him if he is convicted of the crime in a court of law. Fear makes people talk. Another tool the police tried is the polygraph. This brought mixed results. The results of a polygraph test are rarely admissible in court. However, the subjects of the polygraphs showed consistent physical signs that were associated with whether the subject was being truthful or not according to the polygraph machine. John Reid, a polygraph analyst, developed a 9-step system of psychological manipulation that is one of the most popular interrogation systems used today. The steps of this system are confrontation, theme development, stopping denials, overcoming objections, getting the suspect's attention, the suspect loses resolve, alternatives, bringing the suspect into the conversation, and the confession. We will mention each of these briefly when we discuss the interrogation. Remember that the suspect is able to invoke her right to counsel or to remain silent at any point in an interrogation. If that happens, the interrogation must stop immediately.

The interrogation room

An interrogation room is designed to make the suspect uncomfortable. A typical interrogation room is small, with one table, three chairs (1 for suspect; 2 for interrogators), nothing on the walls, and usually an observation mirror. The suspect is usually seated in an uncomfortable chair without access to light switches or thermostats. This increases discomfort and establishes a feeling of dependence.

The interview

The **initial interview** is done to determine guilt or innocence. This is NOT a confrontational interview, but more of a time for the detective (interrogator) to understand how the suspect behaves when in a comfortable situation. The detective will observe the behavior, particularly the eye movements, of the suspect when asked questions that require memory recall or creative thinking. The detective will then ask about the crime and observe the individual to see if her behaviors indicate deception. If they do, the interrogation moves to the next level, which often uses Reid's nine-step system.

Step 1: Confrontation: The detective presents the facts of the case and tells the suspect about the evidence against her. The evidence may or may not be real. Remember that police are allowed to deceive suspects in pursuit of the truth. The interrogator does things to make the suspect uncomfortable, such as moving into the suspect's personal space and stating confidently that the suspect is involved in the case. Fidgeting, grooming herself or licking her lips are all signs that the suspect is being deceptive.

The
Miranda
Warning

You have the right to remain silent. Anything you say can and will be used against you in a court of law. You have the right to speak to an attorney, and to have an attorney present during any questioning. If you cannot afford a lawyer, one will be provided for you at government expense.

Step 2: Theme Development: The interrogator makes up a story of the crime from the suspect's perspective. He will put forward ideas about how and why the crime was committed, how the victim was selected, etc. The purpose of this step is to give the suspect something to use to either justify her actions or as an excuse. If the suspect shows interest in a theme or seems to be agreeing with it, he will continue to develop it. If not, the detective will move on to another theme. The interrogator uses a soft, soothing tone of voice to lull the suspect into a false sense of security.

Step 3: Stopping Denials: The interrogator interrupts all denials. If a suspect is allowed to deny her guilt, her confidence will increase. This keeps the suspect's confidence low and helps keep the suspect quiet so she does not ask for an attorney. The interrogator will take a lack of denials as a positive indicator of guilt.

Step 4: Overcoming Objections: Once the interrogator has developed an appropriate theme, which is one that the suspect relates to, the suspect may offer logic-based objections. These are different than simple denials and are treated differently by the interrogator. An example of a logic-based objection is: "I could never break into a store. My friend had a store that was burglarized and I saw the problems that caused." This provides information to the interrogator that he might be able to turn around and use against the suspect. Logic-based objections sometime end up looking more like an admission of guilt.

Step 5: Getting the Suspect's Attention: By this point in the interview, the suspect is probably frustrated and probably looking for a way out. The interrogator will pretend to the be the suspect's ally, which allows him to capitalize on her insecurity. The interrogator may get very close to the suspect, making gestures of concern, such as a pat on the back.

Step 6: The Suspect Loses Resolve: If the suspect's body language shows that she has given up (head in hands, hunched shoulders, etc.), the interrogator will start leading the suspect toward giving a confession. This involves transitioning from theme development to motive alternatives. At this point, the suspect is basically forced to choose a way she committed the crime. The interrogator will maintain eye contract throughout this step because it increases the stress level of the suspect, as well as her desire to escape. Crying at this point is taken as a positive indicator of guilt.

Step 7: Alternatives: At this point, the interrogator offers two possible motives for some aspect of the crime. One alternative is socially acceptable and the other is morally repugnant, or socially unacceptable. The interrogator will build up each motive until the suspect seems to choose one by nodding her head or showing increased signs of surrender.

Step 8: Bringing the Suspect Into the Conversation: Choosing the alternative is the first step in the suspect confessing to the crime. The detective has at least two witnesses to the confession. At least one will be new to the suspect, which increases her stress level.

Step 9: The Confession: The final step is designed to ensure that the confession will be admissible in court. The interrogator will have the suspect write out a confession or state it on videotape. The suspect confirms that the confession is voluntary, not coerced, and signs the statement in front of the witnesses.

The Tools of Forensic Interviewing

The primary tools used in forensic interviewing are the skills of the interviews. Technology may be used to document the interview, such as video or audio recording or photography, but the primary resource is the interviewer.

The forensic interviewer is a highly skilled professional who has proven his abilities in the following areas:

- Ability to utilize evidence-based protocols and practices

- Familiarity with child development

- Familiarity with the physical and emotional reactions to sexual assault

- Ability to remain neutral and unbiased in emotionally charged situations

- Ability to establish rapport with children and sexual assault victims

- Ability to listen

- Emotionally prepared

Evidence-based protocols and practices

Evidence-based protocols and practices are those that have been proven to be effective in conducting forensic interviews. These protocols and practices are developed based on our knowledge of psychology and also designed to comply with the requirements of the legal system for accepting the results as evidence. They have been proven to be effective and objective in obtaining evidence, so the evidence will stand up in court when presented as evidence in a case.

Familiarity with child development

It is essential that any person responsible for interviewing a child understand the developmental processes of children. Children have different mental capacities and ability to express themselves, based on their age and developmental stage. For example, a four-year old child usually understands the basic difference between the truth and a lie. A forensic interviewer must be able to choose and implement the appropriate interview techniques.

Familiarity with the physical and emotional reactions to sexual assault

Victims of sexual assault may express a range of emotions and physical behaviors at the time they are interviewed. Many victims of sexual assault are ashamed, thinking they brought the assault on themselves by something they did. Some are angry and may lash out. Others may be in denial that anything happened to them. The interviewer must be able to elicit information from the people they are interviewing, regardless of their current state of mind. In order to do this, the interviewer must be able to move the victim past her emotional or physical reaction to obtain valid information about the assault.

Ability to remain neutral and unbiased in emotionally charged situations

The victims of assault, regardless of age, will show strong emotions and may also elicit emotional responses from those assigned to help them. The forensic interviewer must be able to remain objective. Inability to do so might bias the interview if the interviewer strays from the interview protocol, ignores a behavioral signal that is important, or otherwise loses objectivity.

Ability to establish rapport with children and sexual assault victims

Subjects of forensic interviews have been through traumatic events. It is important for the interviewer to be able to gain the trust of the subject so they will relax enough to provide truthful answers to the interviewer's questions. This can be accomplished by finding a common interest, ensuring that the subject understands that the interviewers is there to help solve the crime, and not reacting negatively (or positively) to strong emotional outbursts.

Ability to listen

A good interviewer listens more than he talks. The goal is to gain information from the subject of the interview. This requires the interviewer to listen carefully and ask follow-up questions that may provide clues to what happened. Additionally, people are more likely to talk when the person they talk to is listening intently.

Emotionally prepared

The interviewer must be emotionally prepared to hear horrific things from the people he interviews. If the interviewer is unable to maintain objectivity and emotional distance, it will harm both the interview and the interviewer.

Type of questions

Some basic types of questions are used in interviews. Some are more effective than others. The basic types are open ended/invitational, yes/no or forced choice, and tag/suppositional.

Open-ended questions are also called invitational questions. This means that they invite the subject to answer in whatever way the subject chooses. The answer could be very short of very long. The answers may be descriptive, giving the interviewer information that he might not have otherwise learned. An example of an open-ended question is: "Why is playing the piano your favorite hobby?" An example of an invitational question is: "Tell my why playing the piano is your favorite hobby." The question gives the respondent a chance to say as much or as little as she wants to. This is generally considered the best type of question to ask during an interview.

Forced choice, including yes/no, questions are not as good as open-ended questions. The interviewer will still get some information, but it is limited to whatever answer options are offered. A yes/no question will get you a yes or no answer. This provides a very small amount of information to the interviewer. The answers to these questions are often biased and are particularly inaccurate with young children. The questions encourage guessing and discourage elaboration. A forced choice question may be a multiple choice question. For example, an interviewer may ask the subject if the assailant had a small, medium or large build. The answer will give information on the physical size of the assailant, but no more. Additionally, a forced choice question may not contain the correct answer, so the subject is not able to give an accurate response. These questions are useful in building a general profile of someone or of an event, but do not elicit the nuances, such as body odor, sound of voice, etc. These questions also encourage guessing.

Tag and suppositional questions are not acceptable in a forensic interview. This is because they introduce bias to the respondent's answers. A tag question assumes the answer to the question. For example, "You told your Dad that your brother broke the fish bowl, didn't you?" Suppositional questions assume something took place. For example, "What did you do to break the fish bowl?" These questions do not elicit a response other than the one the interviewer has assumed.

The forensic interview has some other tools that can be helpful in interviews, particularly with children. Dolls and drawings of people are often used to get children to show where some one touched them, whether it was appropriate or not. Children may also be asked to draw an event or a picture of how they are feeling. This can provide the skilled interviewer with additional insight into the events being investigated.

The purpose of the interview

The purpose of the forensic interview is to gather information. The interview is designed to establish the who, when and where of the event, as well as to establish the context of the assault. The context helps establish a clear picture of what happened, when it happened, who was involved, and may offer additional information that corroborates or discredits various versions of the event. The interviewer will try to get as many details as possible about location, the number of times something happened, witnesses, and other information relevant to the crime. The interviewer will also talk to people associated with the victim, such as caretakers, friends, teachers, spouses/significant others, employers, etc., to build a complete picture of the crime. Interviews are close by taking the mind of the victim away from the crime. This can be accomplished by talking about other activities, thanking them for the time they spent being interviewed, and asking the subject about any questions or concerns raised by the interview.

Educational Requirements

A forensic interviewer is likely to be a law enforcement officer or social worker with special training in performing interviews with children or victims of sexual assault. If you are joining the military to gain experience as a forensic interviewer, you need to have a high school diploma and be willing to learn the skills. It is possible to gain certification as a Certified Forensic Interviewer. All applicants must have two to four years of experience in a public or private position responsible for investigation, interviewing, and interrogation. Experience as a full time faculty member at an accredited education institution may also be sufficient.

Anyone who has been convicted of a felony or certain other crimes is ineligible to become a certified forensic interviewer.

The applicant must meet one of the four criteria listed below before taking the certification exam:

- Bachelor's degree or higher plus two years of experience as described above.

- Associate's degree plus three years of experience as described above.

- High school diploma or GED plus four years of experience as state above.

- Minimum of two years of experience as a full time faculty member at an accredited educational institution teaching interview and interrogation techniques.

Summary

Forensic interviewing is a specific type of interviewing designed to gain information from victims of child abuse or adult sexual assault. This type of interviewing is very different from police interrogation. The goal of forensic interviewing is to obtain information from the subject in a non-threatening, objective manner so that it can be used to investigate the crime, as well as for use as evidence in court. A forensic interviewer must be able to remain objective and emotionally detached in order to perform the interview without introducing bias. Interviewers use different types of questions to get information from their subjects. The invitational and open-ended questions are the most useful and the tag and suppositional questions are the least useful. A forensic interviewer has specific training and experience. The educational and experience requirements vary.

· ·

Concept Reinforcement

1. Describe forensic interviewing.

2. Explain why a forensic interviewer must remain objective.

3. Discuss the differences between forced choice and invitational questions.

Chapter 37 – Forensic Engineering

Chapter Objective

- Describe forensic engineering and its applications

Forensic Engineering

Forensic engineering is the application of the art and science of engineering to matters of law. As with other forensic sciences, engineering principles are applied in support of legal activities. Forensic engineers must be experts in their fields, objective during their forensic investigations, and able to testify in court.

Forensic engineers investigate engineered systems, buildings, structures, vehicles, materials, products, structures and components that either fail completely or do not work as they are supposed to. These failures sometimes lead to property damage, and may even lead to personal injury. A forensic engineer works to find the cause(s) of failure. The information gained is generally used for two purposes: to improve the product, or to assist the court in determining the facts in a case.

Some key areas of forensic engineering are accident reconstruction, product liability, structural failures, electrical failures, fires and explosions, and patents.

Accident reconstruction is primarily used to reconstruct vehicle accidents. These accidents can range from simple collisions to multi-vehicle accidents, which can become quite complex. The forensic engineers investigate vehicle speeds, component failure, construction equipment failures, crashworthiness, mechanical design, mechanical equipment failures, occupant kinematics (movement), occupant restraint analysis, vehicle dynamics, and visibility analysis.

This photograph is part of the National Transportation Safety Board accident report for TWA Flight 800 and shows a photograph of the large three-dimensional reconstruction with the support scaffolding visible.
Image courtesy of the National Transportation Safety Board.

Product liability is the area of forensic engineering in which the safety, design, and failure of various products is evaluated. Mechanical and electrical engineers may perform design evaluation, hazard analysis, machine guarding safety analysis, mechanical testing, metallurgical evaluation and assessment, nondestructive testing, product defect and failure analysis, and risk assessment.

Structural failures are examined by civil and structural engineers. In general, these experts analyze structural failures, deficiencies and building envelope distress, which includes air and water leakage. Specific services includes civil and structural failure analysis, construction defect analysis, plumbing and heating failure analysis, building collapses, commercial property damage, foundations, heaving and expansive soils, residential property damage, roofing damage, and slips and falls.

Electrical failures include events that range from the failure of small consumer electronics to complex system failures such as transformer and power plant failures. Forensic electrical engineers also investigate electrical injuries, electrocutions, and the analysis of electrical failures as potential causes of fire. They will also investigate lightning and other power surges, building electrical system failures, and utility power system failures and accidents.

Fire and explosion investigators analyze complex chains of events that involve vehicular, residential and industrial fires and explosions to determine the precise cause and origin of the fire or explosion. These engineers investigate carelessly discarded smoking materials, chemical fires, electrical fires, arson, industrial facility fires, natural gas and LP explosions, power plant explosions and fires that result from spontaneous combustion.

History of Forensic Engineering

The roots of forensic engineering extend far back into human civilization. Civilizations developed codes that imposed penalties on people who built buildings or other engineered systems that failed for some reason. Specific penalties are listed in Hammurabi's Code, the Napoleonic Code, and English Common Law.

> **Stela**
> A stone slab or pillar containing carvings that is usually used for commemorative purposes.

The upper part of the stela of Hammurabi's code of laws

Hammurabi was the king of Babylon about 2,200 BC. Hammurabi is famous for the nature of his penalties: an eye for an eye. In the context of builders, it provides very specific penalties. If the owner of the home is killed by a home structure failure, the builder was to be killed. If eldest son of the homeowner was killed, the eldest son of the builder would be put to death. If a slave of the homeowner was killed, the builder had to give the homeowner a slave of equal value.

Hammurabi's code goes on to say that is the structural failure destroys property, the builder must restore the property AND rebuild the collapsed house at his own expense. Likewise, if he builds a wall that is not strong enough, the builder has to strengthen it as his own expense.

The Napoleonic Code was instituted in France in 1804. The penalties instituted by this code for structural failure are far less extreme than those of Hammurabi. The Napoleonic code imposes a penalty of prison on the contractor and architect of any building that fails within 10 years of its completion. The failure could have been the result of a foundation failure or from poor workmanship.

English Common law from the 15th century was much more vague. All it says is that if a carpenter builds a house poorly, he will be subject to legal action.

Some famous examples of failures are the Tower of Pisa and the 1981 Hyatt Regency walkway failure

The Tower of Pisa is in Italy. You may have heard it described as the leaning Tower of Pisa. Since its construction, it has begun to lean so it is no longer standing upright. The tower is about 60 meters (200 feet) tall and is inclined 5.5° from center. Efforts have been ongoing since 1173 to determine the cause of the problem, as well as to correct it. None have been successful to date.

Third floor walkway of the Kansas City Hyatt Regency, and remaining poles of second and fourth. Image courtesy of Dr. Lee Lowery, Jr, PE

The Hyatt Regency hotel in Kansas City, Missouri, was opened in July, 1980. In July, 1981, a walkway in the hotel collapsed, killing 114 people who were attending a tea dance. An additional 200 hundred were injured. The lobby of the hotel was an atrium with walkways at each floor. The walkways were full of people watching the tea party, which was really a dance contest, when the walkway collapsed. The cause of the collapse was change in the design that occurred during construction and reduced the ability of walkways to support more than their own weight. Wayne Lischka, a structural engineer, discovered that the design of the walkways was insufficient to support the loads required by Kansas City construction codes.

Concept Extension: Failure

Failure is the reason forensic engineering exists. Anything that is made by humans has the potential to fail. The general definition of failure, in terms of engineering, is the inability of a components, structure or facility to perform its intended function. This does not imply, however, that failure always involves collapse or rupture of a system.

Failure is divided into several classifications: Safety failure, functional failure, and ancillary failure.

Safety failure occurs when people are put at risk of injury or death. It also occurs when death or injury result from the failure. An example is the collapse of a railing if someone puts weight on it.

Functional failure occurs when the intended use of the structure or facility is compromised. A common functional failure occurs when air handling systems do not work properly.

Ancillary failures adversely affect schedules, cost or the intended use of an engineered system. A common example is cost overruns on construction jobs.

About half of failures are the result of design deficiencies. Another 25 percent are the result of construction errors. The remaining 25 percent of failures are the result of material defects (~15%) and maintenance deficiencies (~10%).

The Tools of Forensic Engineering

The primary tool of forensic engineers is their expertise. In order to perform their engineering analyses, forensic engineers use a number of tools. Forensic engineers use a wide range of tools, including measuring devices, photographic equipment, clothing, data recording tools, sample collection tools, lights, lanterns, calculators, small hand tools, ladders, scaffolding, and hoists.

- Measuring devices include a basic measuring tape, crack measuring devices, and surveyor's and carpenter's levels.

- Photographic equipment includes still and video cameras with the appropriate film, lenses, data chips, tripods, filters, flashes, and power sources.

- The engineering team will need coveralls, gloves, hats, raincoats, sun shades, boots, and other clothing appropriate to the site conditions.

- Data recording equipment includes a basic clipboard with paper and a pen, an audio records, and blueprints, if they are available.

- Other tools include sample collection (bags and plastic containers), lights, lanterns, calculators, small hand tools, and ladders of varying sizes.

Certain sites may require scaffolding and hoists to allow the investigators to get to the different parts of the scene. In the case of really big structural failures, like what happened with the World Trade Towers, heavy equipment will be brought in to move rubble from the scene.

This image shows the grid on the floor of the RLV Hangar as workers in the field bring in pieces of Columbia's debris. The Columbia Reconstruction Project Team is attempting to reconstruct the bottom of the orbiter as part of the investigation into the accident that caused the destruction of Columbia and the loss of its crew as it returned to Earth on mission STS-107. Image courtesy of NASA

In addition to the basic tools, forensic engineers are able to take advantage of advances in modern technology for their laboratory tests. One of the newer technologies is forensic animation. Forensic animation is used to recreate incidents to help investigators. Forensic animation may be accomplished using computer animation, still photos, and other audiovisual aids. Experts in this field provide scientifically accurate graphics and animations for use in the courtroom. Forensic animation includes real-time simulation, 3D modeling, photo matching, photogrammetry, video matching, videogrammetry, visual analysis, development of court exhibits and graphics, and interactive presentations.

The investigation

Forensic engineers use the scientific method to perform their studies. When a forensic engineer is asked to investigate an accident scene, they follow the scientific method.

The first step is the investigation, in which the team makes observations and tests the hypotheses they develop based on their observations. The team consists of people when appropriate expertise, such as specific engineering disciplines, photographers, and test specialists.

Once the team is assembled, they will visit the site of the accident. While at the site, they will carefully plan the investigation and document all of their findings.

They will collect samples, ensuring complete documentation and cataloging of the samples. The team will also document the scene itself, using photographs, sketches, and notes. Eyewitness accounts are also critical to the scene documentation.

Once the forensic engineering team has collected all of the evidence and documentation, it will develop and test a hypothesis of the failure. This is done by examining photos, design calculations, and other evidence, and conducting structural and laboratory tests.

The team will prepare its conclusions once it has completed its analysis. The report will state probable causes for the failure and provide support for the team's conclusions.

Educational Requirements

A forensic engineer must be a professional engineer, meaning that she has completed an engineering degree and be registered as a professional engineer. In addition to the engineering credentials, a forensic engineer must understand how to perform an investigation, and prepare and present evidence in court.

Summary

Forensic engineering is the application of the art and science of engineering to matters of law. Forensic engineers investigate failures. These include failures in large engineered systems, such as buildings, vehicle crashes, power system failures, and so on. Forensic engineers also analyze failures of consumer electronics, components of products, and materials.Forensic engineers use a number of common tools in doing their investigations. They also follow the scientific method when performing their investigations to ensure that the findings of the investigation are admissible in court.

. . . .

Concept Reinforcement

1. Describe forensic engineering.

2. Explain why forensic engineers follow the scientific method.

3. Discuss what forensic engineers analyze when performing a vehicular accident reconstruction.

Chapter 38 – Digital Forensics

Chapter Objective

- Describe digital forensics and its applications

Digital Forensics

Digital forensics is also known as computer forensics. Digital forensics is the application of digital and computer technologies to matters of law. Every keystroke you make on a computer leaves a trail, which is traceable by an expert in digital/computer forensics. Every web site you visit and every email and text message you send is traceable. The information left behind is called digital artifacts. Digital artifacts may also include an entire computer system, a document or other computer files, or the path the message took as it moved across the Internet.

Digital forensics is used in legal cases, often to analyze computer systems belonging to parties to the court action. These could be criminal or civil cases. Digital forensics are also useful in analyzing how hackers gain access to secure system and what the hacker did to the system. It may also be used to gather evidence against users of the computer system if there are signs of misbehavior.

Category	Type of case
Criminal Prosecutions	Child pornography Homicides Embezzlement Financial Fraud
Civil Litigation	Fraud Divorce Breach of Contract Copyright
Insurance Companies	False accident reports Worker's compensation
Large Corporations	Embezzlement Insider Trading
Law Enforcement	Investigations
Any Individual	Sexual Harassment Age Discrimination Wrongful Termination Background Check

Other uses of computer forensics are data recovery in the event of hardware or software failures and learning how computer systems function in order to increase performance, find errors, or reverse-engineer a system you wish to duplicate or understand better.

Those who are first to respond to a crime scene that contains digital evidence must be extremely careful about how the evidence is handled. The courts scrutinize the methods used to handle digital evidence very closely because it is so easy to alter, damage or destroy the original evidence.

Digital evidence

Digital evidence is another form of latent evidence, just like fingerprints and DNA. Latent evidence is evidence that we cannot see, but which is important to the resolution of a case. Digital evidence must be gathered from the computers and other devices that hold it using specialized equipment and expertise. Digital evidence is also very fragile. This means that very specific protocols must be followed to ensure the evidence is not damaged.

How is digital evidence collected and processed?

In general, the procedures used with digital evidence follow four basic phases: collection, examination, analysis and reporting.

Collection: This phase includes the search for evidence, recognition of evidence, collection of evidence, and documentation of electronic evidence. This phase is critical to ensure that any real-time and stored informationis collected before it is lost. The key steps in handling electronic evidence at the scene are:

- Recognition and identification of digital evidence.

- Documentation of the crime scene.

- Collection and preservation of the evidence.

- Packaging and transportation of the evidence.

It is important to know that, just like other evidence, electronic evidence may be protected by federal law. It is important to make sure you have the legal authority to access data before actually doing so.

Examination: In this phase, the evidence is made "visible" and its origin and significance are explained. Two primary goals are achieved during this phase:

- Documentation of the content and state of the evidence in its totality. This includes a search for any hidden information and allows everyone to know what the evidence contains.

- Data reduction, which is the process of separating the useful data from the rest of the data.

Analysis: In this phase, investigators look at the data they determined is viable forensic evidence to determine if it is significant and supports the case. This is a technical review of the evidence, the notes from which must be preserved for use in legal proceedings, such as discovery or testimony.

Reporting: A written report is prepared the details the protocols used to examine the evidence, as well as the relevant data recovered during the investigation.

Keep in mind that the digital forensics expert will probably be called to testify in court regarding her qualifications to conduct the exam, the conduct of the exam, and the findings of the exam.

Digital Crimes

There are several categories of computer crime that are investigated by computer forensics experts. These include on-line auction fraud, child exploitation and abuse, computer intrusions, death investigation, domestic violence, economic fraud (on-line fraud and counterfeiting), email threats, email harassment and stalking, extortion, gambling, identity theft, narcotics, prostitution, software piracy, and telecommunications fraud. As you can see, this is a wide range of crimes. Digital forensics play a key role in investigating a wide range of crime because of the extent to which computers and other electronics are used when committing crime.

Doctored Images

Doctored images have long been used to present a false image to the public. Historic figures, such as Stalin, had images doctored to make themselves look more heroic or to remove parts of the images that they considered detrimental to their reputations. This has gotten much easier with the advances in computer technology and image manipulation software. Falsified images can be used to present inaccurate scientific data and misrepresent events and people. In the context of the court system, cases involving child pornography, for example, rely heavily on images. The field of digital image forensics is a young, but rapidly growing, discipline.

History of Digital Forensics

Digital forensics is a young field of forensic sciences, which really started gaining importance as the personal computer made its way into workplace and the homes of people all over the world. Michael Anderson, a special agent with the Internal Revenue Service, is considered the father of computer forensics.

A brief timeline of the discipline is below.

Year	Event
1984	FBI Magnetic Media Program created. This later became the Computer Analysis and Response Team (CART)
1988	The International Association of Computer Investigative Specialists (IACIS) created. First Seized Computer Evidence Recovery Specialists (SCERS) classes held.
1993	First International Conference on Computer Evidence
1995	International Organization on Computer Evidence (IOCE) formed.
1997	The G8 countries declared the importance of law enforcement personnel being trained and equipped to address high tech crimes. The Moscow Communiqué of December.
1998	INTERPOL Forensic Science Symposium – G8 countries appoint a committee to create international principles for the procedures used to manage digital evidence.
1999	FBI CART caseload exceeds 2,000 cases, including 17 terabytes of data.
2000	First FBI regional computer forensic laboratory established
2003	FBI CART caseload exceeds 6,500 cases, including 782 terabytes of data.

Concept Extension: Types of Digital Evidence

Many types of devices contain digital evidence, including computer systems, computer components, access control devices, answering machines, digital cameras, handheld devices, hard drives, memory cards, modems, network components, pagers, printers, removable storage devices and media, scanners, telephones, other miscellaneous electronic items. The table below shows the type of digital evidence, subsets of that evidence, primary uses, and primary evidence contained. This table is adapted from the US Department of Justice's Electronic Crime Scene Investigation Guide for First Responders.

Type of Digital Evidence	Subsets of Type of Digital Evidence	Primary Uses	Primary Evidence
Computer System	User-Created Files User-Protected Files Computer-Created Files Other Data Areas	All types of computing functions and information storage (word processing, calculations, communications, graphics)	Files stored on hard drives, storage devices, and media
Computer Components	Central Processing Units (CPUs) Memory	Performs all arithmetic and logical functions in the computer, as well as controlling the computer's operations. Stores the user's programs and data while the computer is in operation.	Evidence of component theft, counterfeiting, remarking.
Access Control Devices	Smart Cards Dongles Biometric Scanners	Access control to computers or programs Functions as an encryption key	Identification/ authentication information of the card and the user Level of access Configurations Permissions The device itself
Answering Machines	-----	Records voice message form callers when the call is not answered.	Voice messages Time and date information Caller ID information Deleted messages Last number called Memo Phone numbers and names Tapes
Digital Cameras	-----	Capture images and/or video in a digital format that is easily transferred to computer storage media for viewing and editing.	Images Removable cartridges Sound Time and date stamp Video

Handheld Devices	Personal Digital Assistants (PDAs) Electronic Organizers	Handheld computing Storage Communication devices capable of storing information	Address book Appointment calendar/ information Documents Email Handwriting Password Phone book Text messages Voice messages
Hard Drives	-----	Information storage, including computer programs, text, video, pictures, multimedia files, etc.	Files stored on hard drives, storage devices, and media
Memory Cards	-----	Additional removable methods of storing and transporting information	Files stored on hard drives, storage devices, and media
Modems	-----	Facilitates electronic communication by allowing a computer to access other networks via a telephone line, wireless, fiber optic, Ethernet, or other communications medium.	The modem device
Network Components	Local Area Network (LAN) card Network Interface Card (NIC) Routers Hubs Switches Servers Network Cables Connectors	LAN and NIC cards connect computers and allow information exchange and resource sharing. Routers, hubs and switches distribute and facilitate the distribution of data through networks. Servers provide shared resources, including e-mail, web and print services for a network. Cables and connectors connect computer components.	LAN/NIC Cards: The device Media Access Control Routers, hubs, and switches: The devices, as well as configuration files from the routers. Servers: Files stored on hard drives, storage devices, and media Cables/Connectors: the devices.

Pagers	-----	Sending and receiving electronic messages in numeric and alphanumeric formats	Address information E-mail Phone numbers Text messages Voice messages
Printers	-----	Print text, images, and other files from a computer.	Usage logs Documents Hard drive Ink cartridges Network identity/ information User usage log Time and date stamp Superimposed images on the roller.
Removable Storage Devices and Media	-----	Portable devices for storing computer programs, text, pictures, video, multimedia files, etc.	Files stored on hard drives, storage devices, and media
Scanners	-----	Converts documents, including images, to electronic files.	The device itself. Ability to scan may help prove an illegal activity. Imperfections on scanner may allow for unique identification of a scanner used to process documents.
Telephones	-----	Two-way communication, as well as some data storage.	Appointment calendars/ information Caller ID Electronic Serial Number E-mail Memo Password Phone book Text messages Voice mail Web browsers
Copiers	-----	Document duplication.	Time/date stamp User usage log Documents
Credit Card Skimmers	-----	Read information from the magnetic stripe on credit cards	Card expiration date Card number User's address User's name

Digital Watches	-----	Tell time. Store additional information, such as address books, calendars, email and notes.	Address book Appointment calendar E-mail Notes Phone Numbers
Facsimile Machines	-----	Store preprogrammed numbers and history of documents sent and received. May include documents held in memory.	Documents Film cartridge Phone numbers Send/receive log
Global Positioning Systems (GPS)	-----	Information on previous travel. Travel logs.	Home Previous destination Travel logs Way point coordinates Way point name.

The Tools of Digital/Computer Forensics

A digital forensic investigation requires a specific tool kit. Some of the tools are the same as those used by other forensic investigators. Others are specific to working with electronic devices.

Documentation tools include cable tags, permanent felt tip markers, and adhesive labels.

Disassembly and removal tools must all be nonmagnetic because of the danger of destroying data. These tools are used to take apart computer systems and components. Tools include flat and Philips screwdrivers, hex-nut drivers, needle nose pliers, secure-bit drivers, small tweezers, specialized screwdrivers, standard pliers, star-type nut drivers, and wire cutters.

Package and transport supplies include anti-static bags and bubble wrap, cable ties, evidence bags and tape, packing materials that do not product static electricity, packing tape and sturdy boxes.

Other basic tools include gloves, a hand truck, large rubber bands, contact list, magnifying glass, printer paper, seizure disk, small flashlight, and unused disks of various types (CDs, DVDs, and floppy disks (3 ½ inch and 5 ¼ inch)).

Software: Digital forensic investigators also use electronic tools to do their investigations. Two key pieces of software are the Encase Forensics Software and the Paraben Mail Examiner. Encase Forensics Software is the most widely used forensic software. It is used by the FBI, Air Force Office of Special Investigations, Scotland Yard, and the US Navy. The Paraben Mail Examiner is designed to recover e-mail.

Educational Requirements

People interested in pursuing digital/computer forensics as a career will probably need to obtain a computer forensics degree, or something related, such as computer science, criminal justice, or engineering, with computer forensics training. Advanced degrees are available, as well, if you wish to pursue them. It is possible to obtain certification in the field of computer forensics. The Certified Electronic Evidence Collection Specialist Certification (CEECS) is awarded to people who complete the CEECS regional certification course and those in the Certified Computer Examiner course that pass the written exam.

Summary

Digital forensics is a young, rapidly growing forensic science. Digital forensics is the application of digital and computer technologies to matters of law. Digital, or computer forensic investigators identify, collect and analyze digital and computer evidence. They follow specific protocols, just like professionals in the other forensics sciences. The four primary phased of a computer forensics investigation are collection, examination, analysis and reporting. All of these steps must be performed with the end goal of giving evidence in court. Digital evidence is fragile and must be handled and analyzed carefully.

Concept Reinforcement

1. Describe computer/digital forensics.

2. Give four characteristics of digital evidence.

3. List four applications of digital forensics in criminal investigations and four applications of the field in civil cases.

Chapter 39 – Forensic Accounting

Chapter Objective

- Describe forensic accounting and its applications

Forensic Accounting

Forensic accounting combines accounting, auditing and investigative skills in the context of the legal system. Forensic accountants use their skills while conducting an investigation, as well as to clearly communicate their findings in a courtroom setting.

Forensic accounting has two sub-disciplines: litigation support and investigative accounting.

Litigation Support provides accounting support to ongoing litigation. The primary goal is to quantify (put into numbers) the economic damages sustained in a specific case, such as the economic loss that might result from a breach of contract.

The role of a forensic accountant in providing litigation support consists of:

- Helping obtain the documentation necessary for the investigation.

- Reviewing the documentation to develop an initial assessment and identify areas of financial loss

- Assisting with the development of questions to be asked regarding the financial evidence

- Attending legal proceedings to review testimony, help the participants understand the financial issues, and develop more questions regarding the financial evidence.

- Reviewing the damages report developed by the opposing legal team, including identifying and reporting on strengths and weakness of the report.

- Assist with settlement discussions and negotiations.

- Attending the trial to listen to testimony and assist with cross-examination.

Investigative Accounting is used to investigate criminal matters. The primary goal is to determine whether a financial crime has occurred. Some examples include embezzlement (theft from the company), money laundering, securities or insurance fraud, and kickbacks. Investigative accounting is becoming increasingly important to anti-terrorist investigations, tracking drug funds, and other international criminal activities.

Forensic accountants can help in criminal investigations by reviewing the facts at hand and providing suggestions about courses of action. They can also assist with the protection and recovery of assets, either by way of civil action or criminal prosecution. They may also coordinate other experts, including consulting engineers, forensic document examiners and private investigators.

Forensic accountants must be able to analyze, interpret, summarize and clearly present complex financial and business information.

The primary roles of forensic accountants are:

- Investigating and analyzing financial evidence

- Developing computerized applications to help with analyzing and presenting financial evidence.

- Present their findings using reports, exhibits, and document collections.

- Assisting with legal proceedings, including providing testimony in court and preparing visual aids for use in the trial.

- A forensic accountant may be asked to help with a wide variety of cases.

Type of Case	Role
Criminal Investigations	Assist with the financial aspects of a criminal investigation. Present evidence in court in a professional and concise manner.
Shareholders' and Partnership disputes	Perform a detailed analysis of business accounts spanning several years to quantify the issues in the dispute.
Personal Injury Claims and Motor Vehicle Accidents	Quantify the economic losses to the victim of a motor vehicle accident, medical malpractice, and wrongful dismissal from a job.
Business Interruption/Other Insurance Claims	Perform detailed reviews of business insurance policies to investigate the coverage issues and determine the appropriate way to calculate the loss.
Business/Employee Fraud Investigations	Assist with tracing funds, identifying and recovering lost assets, gathering forensic intelligence, and performing due diligence reviews.
Marital Disputes	Trace, locate and evaluate assets. The assets may be business, properties, jewelry, or other assets.
Business Economic Losses	Investigate contract disputes, construction claims, expropriations, product liability claims, trademark and patent infringements, and losses resulting from the breach of non-competition agreements.
Professional Negligence	Determine if a breach of standards of accounting practice have occurred and quantify the resulting losses.
Mediation and Arbitration	Provide alternate dispute resolution services to resolve disputes with minimal disruption and cost (financial and time).

History of Forensic Accounting

The use of accountants as expert witnesses can be traced back to 1817 and the court decision of Meyer v. Sefton. In this case, which was about the valuation of a bankrupt person's estate, an accountant was allowed to testify in court. The earliest reference to forensic accounting appears in an advertising circular dating back to Glasgow, Scotland, in 1824.

Mug shot of gangster Al Capone.

The first known use of forensic accounting in the US was in the conviction of Al Capone in the 1931. The legal system was unable to arrest or convict him based on the obvious crimes he committed: murder, bootlegging, etc. The IRS did finally arrest and convict him for tax evasion. The FBI employed nearly 500 forensic accountants during World War II. Since then, the field has grown significantly, in large part because of the implementation of new accounting practices and tax laws.

Year	Event
1817	First accountant testified in court in Meyer v. Sefton
1931	Al Capone was arrested by the IRS for tax evasion.
1942	Maurice E. Peloubet published "Forensic Accounting: Its place in today's economy."
1982	Francis C. Dykman published "Forensic Accounting: The Accountant as an Expert Witness."
1986	The AICPA issued Practice Aid #7. This outlines six areas of litigation services: damages, antitrust analysis, accounting, valuation, general consulting, analyses.
1988	Association of Certified Fraud Examiners established.
1992	The American College of Forensic Examiners was founded.
1997	The American Board of Forensic Accountants was founded.
2000	The Journal of Forensic Accounting, Auditing, Fraud and Taxation was founded.

Concept Extension: The Forensic Accounting Investigation

Most forensic accounting investigations follow a similar pattern, which we will go through here.

Step in the process	Purpose
Client meeting	Get to know the people involved, available facts, and the issues of the case.
Conflict of interest check	Be sure that the forensic accountant does not have a conflict of interest with any of the parties involved.
Preliminary Investigation	An initial investigation will help the forensic accountant develop a plan of action for the investigation based on a better understanding of the issues of the case.

Develop an action plan	Set the objectives of the overall investigation, including determining the appropriate methodology to be used.
Obtain evidence	Gather the evidence required for the investigation. This may include documents, economic data, assets, people, companies, other experts, and proof of the occurrence of an event.
Perform the analysis	The actual analysis used will depend on the nature of the assignment. The analyses may include: Calculating economic damages. Summarizing a large number of transactions. Tracing assets. Calculating present value using appropriate discount rates. Performing regression and sensitivity analyses. Using computerized tools, such as spread sheets, databases and computer models. Use charts and graphics to explain the analysis.
Prepare the report	Prepare a report summarizing the findings of the investigation and providing supporting detail. The report will contain information on the nature of the assignment, the scope (including limitations) of the investigation, the investigative and analytical approaches used, and the findings of the investigation. Supporting detail includes financial schedules, graphics, and other details necessary to support and explain the findings.

The Tools of Forensic Accountants

The primary tool of the forensic accountant is his understanding of accounting and methods for investigating financial transactions. Technical tools associated with financial accounting are primarily software packages that allow the investigators to analyze the financial information found during their investigations.

Educational Requirements

A person interested in becoming a forensic accountant should begin by obtaining a bachelor's degree in accounting. The next step is to take the certified public accountant (CPA) exam. CPAs are held to higher standards than others because they have a social obligation that goes beyond the client-accountant relationship. Forensic accountants are required to adhere to even higher standards than the AICPA (certification organization for CPAs) requires of CPAs. Forensic accountants must remain independent and objective when analyzing and reporting on economic transactions.

Summary

Forensic accounting is a relatively new field of forensic sciences. The forensic accountant applies accounting principles and practices in the context of the legal system. Forensic accountants work in two primary areas: litigation support and investigative accounting. Investigative accounting may be performed in the context criminal or civil cases, and may also be performed for businesses and insurance purposes.

Concept Reinforcement

1. Describe forensic accounting.

2. State the goal of investigative accounting.

3. List the four primary roles of a forensic accountant.

218

Chapter 40 – Animal Investigators

Chapter Objective

- Describe the importance of animal examiners in crime scene investigation

Animal Investigators

Dogs are probably the best known of the animals used to help investigate crime scenes. Dogs have incredibly sensitive hearing and senses of smell. They are able to track people, detect drugs and bombs, and alert their handlers. People benefit from dogs trained to assist the disabled, perform search-and-rescue mission, detect bombs and drugs, and as key parts of the police force.

Dogs have significant advantages over humans. A dog's sense of smell is about 50 times more sensitive than that of a human. In addition, a dog is better able to differentiate between scents and detect a specific one even in the presence of dozens of other scents.

A police dog and his handler
Image courtesy of the US Senate

Dogs are often able to perform these tasks much more accurately and efficiently than humans. In fact, a 1990 study conducted for the police department in Lansing, Michigan, found that a single K-9 team (dog and handler) is able to complete a building search about seven times faster than four officers working together. The dog team also found hidden suspects 93% of the time, compared to a success rate of 59% for the human team.

Police dogs are used as animal investigators in a number of situations, including searches for dead bodies, search and rescue, finding victims and criminals, controlling criminals, article searches, and other situations in which the dogs particular skills will help find evidence in a crime. They are even used to help locate crime scenes.

History of Animal Investigators

Dogs were first domesticated more than 15,000 years ago. They were initially used for hunting, hauling and guarding. Eventually, people began to exploit the aggressiveness of dogs for war purposes. These war dogs were typically part of the forward attack elements of an army. Dogs were also used for internal control within organizations. They were useful in controlling slaves and guarding property. Use of dogs for protection and as soldiers continues through the present day.

European police organizations were the first to use dogs in law enforcement in an organized way. This began in the early 1900s and was largely the result of efforts by purebred dog clubs. England, Germany and Belgium led the way in developing dogs as members of the law enforcement team.

The Military Working Dog Program was established by the US Army in 1942. This occurred after the Japanese attack on Pearl Harbor. Dogs were first used as sentries, meaning they were responsible for guarding military personnel and resources. The military then began using dogs as scouts. The dogs would help the soldiers avoid the enemy.

A Marine with the 7th War Dog Platoon, 25th Marine Regiment, takes a nap while Butch, his war dog, stands guard. Iwo Jima, February 1945.
Staff Sergeant M. Kauffman, USMC

After World War II, the Japanese found that sentry dogs were far more effective at securing warehouses than human guards. Sixty-five sentry dogs could secure warehouses and there were no losses. When 600 men guarded the same warehouses, more than $600,000 of inventory was lost.

When the US entered the Korean War, the Army had about 100 sentry dogs and one scout dog platoon on the ground in Korea. After the Korean War was over, the Air Force had increased need for guard dogs to protect missile sites and air force bases. Sentry and scout dogs were again important during the Vietnam War, where they were widely used. Dogs were also trained to detect mines and tunnels and to track the enemy.

The Air Force changed the role of the military dog beginning in 1968 when they began to train dogs for patrol rather than sentry duty. Patrol dogs were more manageable and versatile than sentry dogs and more like our modern police dogs.

Trained attack dog Samo leaps forward toward a decoy's arm wrap as
Tech. Sgt. David Adcox restrains him. U.S. Air Force photo/Robbin Cresswell

The military has used dogs for a number of purposes, including as sentries, scouts, trackers, and casualty and cadaver dogs. Dogs continue to play an important role in US military operations.

WORKING DOG — U.S. Air Force military working dog Jackson sits on a
U.S. Army M2A3 Bradley Fighting Vehicle before heading out on a mission in
Kahn Bani Sahd, Iraq, Feb. 13, 2007. His handler is Tech. Sgt. Harvey Holt,
of the 732nd Expeditionary Security Forces Squadron.
U.S. Air Force photo by Staff Sgt. Stacy L. Pearsall

Historically, police dogs have not been used for crime scene investigations. It is, however, becoming more common as the handlers and police forces realize the advantages of using the dogs to find bodies, track victims and perpetrators, and locate crime scenes.

Concept Extension: Which type of dog is best for the job?

There are many different breeds of dogs in the world. They come in many shapes and sizes. Some are intimidating, like the German Shepherd or the Doberman. Others are cute and cuddly and not likely to intimidate anyone, no matter how fierce the dogs think they are. Think of Yorkshire terriers and toy poodles. They are not likely to instill fear. Other considerations when choosing a police service dog are intelligence, aggression, strength and sense of smell.

The standard image of a police dog is as a public order enforcement dog. These are the dogs that chase and hold suspects, or even prevent suspects from fleeing because of the threat of being chased down by the dog. German Shepherds and Belgian Malinois are the most commonly used breeds. However, other breeds, such as Dutch Shepherds, Rottweilers, Doberman Pinschers, American Pit Bull Terriers and American Staffordshire terriers have served as police service dogs.

Illicit substance detection breeds: The German Shepherd, Belgian Malinois, beagle, basset hound, fox hound, and Laborador retriever

Tracking breeds: bloodhounds and coonhounds are good at tracking missing people or items.

Cadaver sniffing dogs: Beagles and bloodhounds

Police Service Dogs in Crime Scene Investigation

Police Service Dogs can be of great assistance to the crime scene investigator. Trained dogs are able to track victims and suspects, locate the crime scene, find lost items, and locate drugs and explosives.

Tracking and article search are two key skills of a canine team. Tracking is just what it sounds like. The dog locates a scent trail and follows it, hopefully finding a person or the crime scene. Article search behavior occurs when you use the scent on an article or group of articles in an attempt to locate the crime scene.

Scent Material

Scent material is anything that carries the scent of a suspect or a victim and that can be used to try to find that person.

The scent material collected at a crime scene can be used for a number of purposes, some of which we have already discussed. These include trailing the subject or finding the subject. This material can also be used to identify a subject in a line-up and may even establish probable cause for a search warrant or arrest.

Scent evidence is the only evidence that can do the following:

- Take you in a direction that is away from the crime scene.

- Give you a path to follow to search for other items related to the crime.

- Lead you to footprints or tire prints, which can then be collected.

- Lead you to a subject and identify the individual.

Scent material is often used in search and rescue missions. A search and rescue dog is given a scent from a piece of clothing or other personal item of the missing person. The dog then attempts to find the person. In some cases, search dogs are fitted with special collars that have cameras and transmitters on them so the search team can monitor what the dog is seeing as he performs his search.

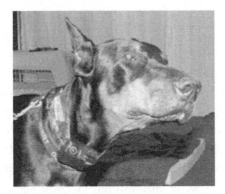

A search dog at Ground Zero following the September 11, 2001 collapse of the World Trade Center is fitted for a TV camera and transmitter.
Image courtesy of FEMA.

Cadaver dogs are specially trained to identify the odor of decomposing bodies and lead the search team to the body. This is useful for bodies that are above ground, in shallow graves, and even in the water. It is less useful for bodies that are deeply buried because the scent does not come up through the ground so the dog can smell it.

Drug dogs are trained to sniff out illegal drugs. They are very successful in doing this because of their ability to differentiate individual scents from many scents. Drug dealers often try to mask the scent of the drugs with other fragrant items, such as coffee beans. Dogs are still able to identify the drugs.

Interestingly, Bomb-sniffing dogs are heavily used in security situations. They are trained to find explosive substances, such as dynamite and chromium. They are also able to detect tiny traces of ammunition residue from guns. They are also able to detect minute traces of explosives. Some dogs are also trained to detect accelerants that are used in arson.

An explosives-detecting dog screening baggage before it goes on an airplane.
Image courtesy of the Transportation Safety Administration

Summary

Animal investigators are crucial to law enforcement. Dogs have proven to be particularly useful because of their extraordinary senses of smell and hearing. The military has forces used dogs for thousands of years. Military (or war) dogs are responsible for guarding people and resources, scouting, and detecting mines and tunnels. Police organizations began using dogs in the early 1900s and K-9 units were soon used by police forces around the world. Animal investigators are used to detect illegal drugs and explosives. They also play an important role in search and rescue operations. Crime scene investigators benefit from trained canines to find victims and criminals, crime scenes, explosives, weapons, drugs, and other scent-based evidence. The breed of dog selected is based on the traits needed for the job. Tracking dogs are often bloodhounds or coonhounds. Public order enforcement dogs are often of the species associated with police dogs – German Shepherds, Dobermans and other dogs that intimidate people. Canine animal investigators must be able to track and do article searches. Dogs can find scent evidence that is not apparent to humans and can be crucial to solving a case.

. . . .

Concept Reinforcement

1. State the advantages of animal investigators in crime scene investigation.

2. List the four unique things scent evidence can do in a crime scene investigation.

3. List and describe the two key skills of a canine investigator.

Chapter 41 – Case Study: The O.J. Simpson Murder Trial

Chapter Objective

- Case Study -Murder - OJ Simpson Case

The O.J. Simpson Murder Case

One of the most notorious criminal trials in history was the 1994 murder trial of OJ Simpson. Simpson was a former American football star and actor that was arrested for the murder of his ex-wife Nicole Brown Simpson and her friend Ronald Goldman. Amongst great controversy, he was acquitted in 1995 after a lengthy trial.

OJ Simpson in 1990

The Crime

Nicole Brown Simpson and Ronald Goldman were found stabbed to death on the evening of June 12th, 1994 at approximately 11:40pm. The bodies were discovered at Nicole's condominium in the Brentwood area of Los Angeles, California. Nicole was stabbed numerous times in the neck and her face was extremely swollen. Ronald Goldman was stabbed multiple times as well. Nicole's dog was found with blood on its paws barking at the crime scene by neighbors at around 11:00pm. Evidence collected at the scene suggested that OJ Simpson was the perpetrator of the crime. Simpson was supposed to turn himself in on the morning of June 17th, but he failed to show up. Police set out to arrest Simpson for two counts of felony murder. Simpson's white Bronco was spotted on the Interstate with his friend Al Cowlings driving. Cowlings indicated that Simpson had a gun to his own head so police followed in a low-speed chase for over 50 miles back to OJ Simpson's residence in Brentwood. Simpson then surrendered to the authorities.

The Trial

Simpson led police on a 50 mile low-speed chase before turning himself in to authorities.

Simpson hired a high-profile team of defense attorneys that were dubbed by the media as the "dream team." The team included F. Lee Bailey, Robert Shapiro, Alan Dershowitz, Robert Kardashian, and Johnnie Cochran. Barry Scheck and Peter Neufeld were also hired to attempt to discredit the DNA evidence of the prosecution. The trial lasted 8 months with over 150 witnesses taking the stand. The trial began on January 25, 1995 and was televised by Court TV. This made the lawyers and Judge (Lance Ito) pseudo-celebrities with millions tuning in everyday to watch the events of the trial unfold. The prosecution presented evidence of OJ Simpson's history of domestic abuse against Nicole, including a 911 tape of Nicole stating she feared that Simpson was going to physically harm her. Although the prosecution did not have the murder weapon and there were no direct witnesses to the murder, they had a mountain of DNA evidence putting Simpson at the scene of the crime. A Brentwood resident testified to police that she saw Simpson's car speeding away from Nicole's house on the night of the murder and another man claimed to have sold Simpson a 15-inch knife similar to the murder weapon weeks earlier. Unfortunately, both of these individuals sold their stories to the tabloids and thus the prosecution chose not to use their testimony. The DNA evidence was strong against Simpson. Samples from the bloody footprints found leading away from the bodies and on the gate exiting the premises were matched to Simpson's blood suggesting he was injured during the attack. When police arrested Simpson he had a large wound on his middle finger. Simpson's attorneys cross-examined the police criminologist for 8 days questioning the procedures that were followed to obtain the samples. It was uncovered that a police trainee that helped to gather the blood samples had carried them in his lab coat pocket for the entire day before turning it in as an exhibit.

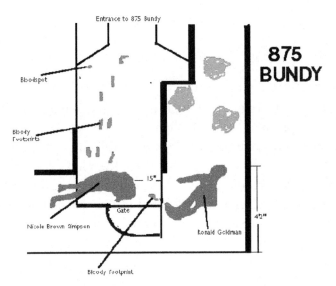

A mockup of the crime scene at Nicole's Brentwood residence

A bloody glove found at Simpson's residence by policeman Mark Fuhrman had blood matching Simpson and both murder victims. The defense attempted to discredit Fuhrman as a racist and claimed he planted all the evidence against Simpson. They utilized tapes from an interview done ten years earlier in which Fuhrman used numerous racial slurs to back up their claim that he was not a credible witness. The prosecution also had Simpson try on the glove used as evidence after the defense team hounded them on the matter. The glove appeared not to fit, but prosecutors argued that the defense purposely had Simpson stop taking his arthritis medication causing his hands to swell. They also pointed out that the glove had shrunken after being soaked in blood and sealed in evidence. The defense used this opportunity and attorney Johnnie Cochran stated the now infamous phrase "if it doesn't fit, you must acquit". Despite the overwhelming amount of evidence presented at the trial, the jury only deliberated for four hours before returning a not guilty verdict on October 3, 1995. Refer to the table below to see a summary of the key evidence presented at trial.

OJ Simpson trying on the bloody gloves found at his residence.

Evidence
9-1-1 Call from Nicole Brown Simpson showing the violent tendency of OJ Simpson in the past.
Hairs consistent with Simpson are found in the cap found at the Bundy crime scene.
Hairs consistent with Simpson are found on the shirt of Ron Goldman.
Fibers consistent with carpet in Simpson's bronco found at Bundy crime scene.
Blood matching Simpsons found near the footprints found at the Bundy crime scene.
Simpson had fresh cuts on his fingers the day after the crime scene.
Blood found in OJ's Bronco, in foyer, master bedroom, driveway and on OJ's socks at his home matching the murder victims.
Left glove found at the crime scene and matching right glove found at Simpson's house.
Shoeprints found at Bundy crime scene matched a pair of size 12 shoes that Simpson was known to have.
Flight away from arrest in Bronco and strange reaction to phone call informing him of Nicole's death.

Evidence presented at Murder Trial of OJ Simpson

Summary

On the night of June 12th, 1994 Nicole Brown Simpson and Ronald Goldman were found brutally stabbed to death outside Nicole's Brentwood residence. Evidence suggested OJ Simpson was the perpetrator of the crime and after a low-speed 50 mile chase police arrested Simpson for double murder. The trial took place over an 8-month time period and was televised on Court TV. Although a mountain of evidence was introduced against Simpson, including DNA evidence, the defense was able to convince the jury of police misconduct. Amongst great controversy, the jury acquitted Simpson of the murders.

Concept Reinforcement

1. What was some of the evidence presented by prosecution at the trial of OJ Simpson?

2. How did defense attorneys attempt to discredit the evidence presented by the prosecution?

3. How long did jurors deliberate before announcing a verdict?

Chapter 42 – Case Study: White Collar Crime – Stock Market Fraud of 2008

Chapter Objective

- Discuss the white collar crime case study on the stock market fraud of 2008

White Collar Crime

White collar crime has been defined as a type of crime that is committed by a person of considerable respectability or high social status in the course of their occupation. This includes corporate crimes such as those involving fraud, embezzlement, bribery, insider trading, forgery, and computer crimes. These crimes involve deceit and not physical violence. Experts have estimated that the costs associated with white collar crimes are approximately 300 billion dollars annually in the United States alone. It is believed that a great deal of white collar crime goes undetected or unreported. Evidence related to white collar crime usually consists of a paper trail or computer files. White collar crime can also be conducted over the course of many years through elaborate schemes. The table below summarizes the most common white collar crimes.

Many white collar crimes involve monetary gain.

Type of Crime	Definition
Bank Fraud	An act or consistent pattern with the purpose of defrauding a bank of funds.
Blackmail	The demand for money or other priority treatment through the use of physical threat or exposure of confidential information.
Bribery	The use of money, goods, or services offered in exchange for personal influence or action of another person or entity. A person can be tried for taking a bribe or offering one.
Cellular Phone Fraud	The illegal tampering or unauthorized use of a cellular phone. This includes stealing the valid ESN number from one cellular phone and transferring it to another.
Computer Fraud	A crime committed by a computer hacker to steal information such as bank account numbers, credit card numbers, or other confidential information.
Counterfeiting	When an individual copies a specific article and attempts to pass it as genuine. This includes money, watches, designer's bags, artwork, or other valuable assets.

Credit Card Fraud	The illegal use of another person's credit card to purchase goods or services.
Embezzlement	When an individual who has been entrusted with a certain amount of money or valuables uses it for their own benefit.
Extortion	When an individual obtains property illegally by threatening force or violence.
Forgery	When an individual passes a fake element such as a check with the intent to defraud the recipient.
Health Care Fraud	When an unlicensed individual provides health care services to others and gains monetarily for the services.
Insider Trading	When an individual uses confidential, non-disclosed information to trade in shares from a public company.
Insurance Fraud	An individual gains monetary benefits by deceiving an insurance company, for instance faking an injury on the job.
Investment Schemes	When an individual promises to gain large returns on a small investment as a ploy to steal money.
Kickback	When an individual sells an item and pays back a portion of the price to the buyer.
Investment Schemes	When an individual promises to gain large returns on a small investment as a ploy to steal money.
Larceny/Theft	The wrongful taking of another person's property.
Investment Schemes	When an individual promises to gain large returns on a small investment as a ploy to steal money.
Money Laundering	The investment or transfer of money gained through illegal activity that is made to appear legitimate.
Racketeering	The engagement in illegal activities (i.e. selling drugs) for personal financial gain.
Securities Fraud	The artificial inflation of a stock price by brokers so individuals will believe they are buying stocks on the rise.
Tax Evasion	When an individual purposely evades paying taxes or falsifies their returns.
Telemarketing Fraud	Individuals place telephone calls to businesses or residences in an attempt to gain monetarily by alleging they are collecting for a charity or other organization.
Welfare Fraud	The act of taking welfare benefits under illegal circumstances.

The Ultimate Ponzi Scheme: Bernie Madoff

One of the most notorious white collar crimes involved the 2008 arrest of **Bernard Madoff** for the operation of one of the largest **Ponzi schemes** in history. A Ponzi scheme is a type of investment scam where an individual solicits the investment of others into a proposed business venture or stock. A high return rate is promised in exchange for the investment.

However, the perpetrator never invests the money and instead appears to pay dividends by using newly recruited investors money. The scheme ends once the scam has run out of new investors to pay old investor dividends or the perpetrator flees town with the money. Bernie Madoff was the owner of one of the largest investment companies, Madoff Securities, and the former chairman of the NASDAQ. His firm was one of the first to begin using computer technology to distribute quotes, which later was applied to the creation of NASDAQ. He began the Ponzi scheme in the early 1990's by offering modest, steady returns to an exclusive group of clients. He produced falsified reports that gave the appearance of successful returns. He defrauded individuals and companies of over 65 billion dollars throughout the course of the scam. The scheme started to unravel in December 2008 when the stock market began to plunge. Panicked investors attempted to withdrawal 7 billion dollars from the firm, which Madoff was unable to pay since the money was never invested. Madoff was arrested and pled guilty of securities fraud, investment advisor fraud, money laundering, and many other white collar crimes. He faces a maximum sentence of 150 years in prison and over $170 billion dollars in fines.

Bernard Madoff was arrested in 2008 for conducting
one of the largest Ponzi schemes in history.

Summary

White collar crimes are committed by person's of considerable respectability or social status in the course of their occupation. White collar crimes involve deception instead of actual physical violence. Approximately 300 billion dollars annually are lost during the commission of white collar crimes in the United States. Bernard Madoff pled guilty to the propagation of one the largest Ponzi schemes in history. He defrauded investors of more than 65 billion dollars over the several decade-long scheme.

Concept Reinforcement

1. Explain how a white collar crime differs from other crimes?

2. Discuss several examples of white collar crimes?

3. Explain how a Ponzi scheme operates.

Chapter 43 – Case Study: Arson – The Unabomber

Chapter Objective

- Discuss the events related to the Unabomber case, including the investigation and arrest of the perpetrator

The Unabomber Case

The search for the man dubbed as the "Unabomber" took place for over 20 years and was one of the most expensive investigations in FBI history. During that time, the **Unabomber** remained on the list as one of America's most wanted criminals. The bombing campaign resulted in 3 deaths and 23 injuries. The attacks did not follow any specific pattern, preventing the authorities from identifying the perpetrator. The bombs that he utilized did have a recognizable signature in that every piece was handmade using items that could be found in any local hardware store. The bomber also included the letters "FC" stamped into some aspect of the metal pieces of the bomb. The bombing campaign lasted from May 1978 until April 1995.

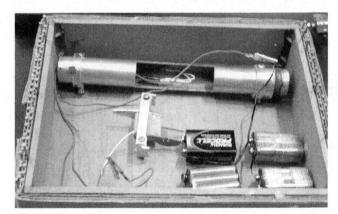

A recreation of one of the bombs used by the Unabomber

The bombings

The first mail bomb was sent in May of 1978 to a materials engineering professor at Northwestern University. The professor was suspicious of the package and reported it to security. A campus policeman opened the package and it exploded immediately. The policeman received only minor injuries. The primary component of the bomb was a metal pipe with a primitive trigger device. More bombs were sent over the next several years to university and airline personnel. One of the bombs in 1979 caused a small fire in the baggage compartment of an American Airlines plane that was in flight to Washington. Fortunately, the devices timing mechanism was faulty preventing it from exploding and killing everyone on board. Over the years, the bombs became more sophisticated and in December 1985 the first fatality occurred as a result of a bombing. A man was seen placing a bomb near a computer store in the beginning of 1987 leading to the famous sketch being produced of the

Unabomber pictured below. The bombings ceased between 1987 and 1993, leading investigators to believe he was incarcerated at the time. The bombing campaign continued in 1993 and by April 1995 had killed two other people. In June 1995, a 35,000 word **manifesto** claiming to be written by the Unabomber was sent to the *New York Times* and *Washington Post*. Included was an announcement that the bombings would cease if the manifesto was published. It was published and the there were no more attacks.

A sketch produced of the Unabomber after he was seen planting a bomb near a computer store in 1987.

Catching the Unabomber

After the Unabomber's manifesto was published, the FBI received thousands of phone calls every day related to the case. Most of these were in response to the one million dollar reward offered for his identification and subsequent arrest. David Kaczynski, read the manifesto in the paper and noted many similarities in the phrasing between letters he had received in the past from his brother and the Unabomber's manifesto. At the encouragement of his wife, he went to the authorities with his suspicions and gave them the letters his brother had sent. Although David had been estranged from his brother, Ted Kaczynski, for over ten years he asked that his identity remain anonymous as the person responsible for identifying the Unabomber. Unfortunately, a leak within the FBI alerted the media who broke the story and reported David as the one who turned in his brother. Ted Kaczynski was arrested on April 3, 1996 at his remote cabin right outside Lincoln, Montana. He was found in a very unkempt state living without running water or electricity. Numerous pieces of evidence were collected in connection with the bombings including bomb making materials and letters similar to the manifesto he wrote. He pled guilty to the bombings and is currently serving a life term in federal prison without the possibility of parole. All his belongings, including his writings, were sold at auction and all proceeds given to the families of the victims. His brother, David, also distributed the reward money amongst the victims.

Ted Kaczynski after his arrest in 1996

Summary

The FBI searched for the identification of the infamous Unabomber for 20 years. The Unabomber's bombing campaign resulted in the death of 3 people and injury of 23 others. Although his pattern was inconsistent as far as targets, his bombs did contain a signature of being handmade with simple supplies from a local hardware store. The Unabomber's 35,000 word manifesto was published in the *New York Times* and *Washington Post* in 1995, in return for the promise of discontinuing the bombings. The writings were recognized by David Kaczynski as similar to the phrasing in letters he received years earlier from his brother. The FBI arrested Ted Kaczynski in April 1996 after which he pled guilty to all the charges and is currently serving a term of life imprisonment with no possibility of parole.

. . . .

Concept Reinforcement

1. Why was it so difficult to identify the Unabomber?

2. What was the signature feature of the Unabomber's devices?

3. How was the Unabomber eventually identified by the FBI?

Chapter 44 – Cold Cases

Chapter Objective

- Describe what entails a cold case and discuss several examples of cold cases

Cold Case

A **cold case** is a crime or accident that has not yet been solved and is currently not the subject of a criminal investigation or civil proceeding. New information can arise that prompts investigators to reopen the case, such as a new witness coming forward or new technologies that have been invented that can be used to test old evidence. Usually cold cases are violent crimes or other felonies that are not subject to a statute of limitations for prosecution of the crime. Disappearances are also considered cold cases when a person has been missing for an extended period of time. Other cases that are classified as cold cases can lead to the exoneration of individuals convicted of a crime they did not commit. With the advent of DNA technology, many cold cases were reopened and the evidence re-examined using the new testing available. This can lead investigators to new suspects that had been previously overlooked. The following section will look at several examples of cold cases that have been solved and others that still remain a mystery today.

A cold case is a crime or accident that has not been solved and is currently not the subject of an active criminal investigation.

Oba Chandler

Oba Chandler

In June 1989, three women were found floating in the Tampa Bay with their hands and feet tied and cement blocks tied around their necks. The autopsies conducted suggested all the women were alive when they were thrown in the water. The investigators in the case used billboards with information and photos of the victims across the Tampa area in hopes that someone had information about the case. This was the first time billboards were used to help in a criminal investigation. The victims were identified as Joan Rogers (36) and her two daughters, Michelle (17) and Christe (14). They were on vacation from their Dairy farm in Ohio and were reported missing by the husband and father of the victims. The case was unsolved for several years with the best pieces of evidence being handwritten directions and a palmprint found on a brochure in the Rogers car. Authorities posted the handwriting from the directions on the billboards and a neighbor of Oba Chandler submitted copy of a work order that Chandler had written. There was a positive match between the two and Chandler became the prime suspect. Chandler was arrested and convicted of the triple murder in 1994.

The disappearance at the Dairy Queen: Cindy Zarzycki

On April 18, 1986 16-year old Cindy Zarzycki left her home and went over her friends to make plans to go to a surprise birthday party for her teen crush, Scott. She left her friends to get a ride to the party at the local Dairy Queen and vanished. For years the case was treated as a teen runaway. The case remained cold for nearly two decades until a new investigator decided to reopen the case and look at the evidence. There was not much to go on, but he decided to go and interview her old crush Scott Ream, only to discover that he had died in a car accidents years earlier. When looking into the background of Scott, investigators discovered his father, Art Ream, had a criminal history of sexual misconduct with minors. He was currently in prison on a rape charge of a minor. Police obtained a warrant to search the residence of Ream where they found a copy of the old missing person's add for Cindy hidden among his belongings. Investigators were able to get Art Ream to finally admit to the crime and lead police to the body of the 16-year old girl. He was convicted of the crime and sentenced to life imprisonment.

16-year old Cindy Zarzycki before she disappeared in 1986.

The Mystery Continues: Natalee Holloway

18-year old Natalee Holloway was on a graduation trip to Aruba when she disappeared on May 30, 2005. She was last seen with three local boys, Jordan Van der Sloot and brothers Deepak and Satish Kalpoe. An extensive search was conducted for Natalie and the case became an instant media sensation. The three boys were all arrested, but they were released due to lack of evidence to charge them with a crime. The body has never been found and the case remains a mystery to investigators.

The disappearance of Natalee Holloway remains a cold case.

Summary

A cold case is a crime or accident that has not yet been solved and is not currently the subject of a criminal investigation. Many cold cases are reopened after new evidence has surfaced such as a new witness. Old cases may also be re-examined to use new technology for testing old evidence that has been preserved in a case. This can help lead investigators to new suspects that had not been questioned previously.

Concept Reinforcement

1. What is a cold case?

2. What reasons could result in a cold case being reopened?

3. What led investigators to suspect Oba Chandler's involvement in the triple murder of three women found in the Tampa Bay?

Chapter 45 – The Innocence Project

Chapter Objective

- Explain the mission of the Innocence Project

The Innocence Project

The **Innocence Project** is a national organization that is dedicated to exonerating individuals that have been wrongly convicted of a crime. The organization utilized DNA testing to help provide evidence that an individual has been wrongly convicted of a crime. The Innocence Project was started in 1992 by attorneys Peter Nuefeld and Barry Scheck. At the headquarters of the Innocence Project clinic, law students help to handle case work free of charge under the supervision of seasoned attorneys.

The Innocence Project works to exonerate individuals that have been wrongly convicted of a crime.

The Process

Most of the clientele of the Innocence Project are poor and have no other resources to turn to for relief. Potential clients of the organization go through a lengthy screening process to determine if DNA evidence could be useful in proving their claims of innocence. Many times when a person is wrongfully convicted of a crime, it is due to witness misidentification, false confessions or faulty forensic work. For example, some individuals have been convicted of crimes based on scientific tests that were not scientifically validated at the time. These include such tests such as bite mark analysis and hair microscopy. In the United States, there have been 235 post-conviction DNA exonerations, many of which are attributed to the work conducted through the Innocence Project.

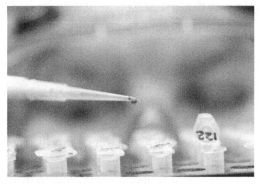

The advent of DNA testing has allowed over 200 wrongly convicted individuals to be released from prison.

Case Profile: Kirk Bloodsworth

Kirk Bloodsworth was convicted in 1985 of the brutal rape and murder of a nine year old girl. An anonymous caller told police they saw Kirk in the area during the day of the murder in June 1984. He was arrested and sentenced to two life terms of imprisonment and the death penalty. DNA testing on evidence from the crime was conducted in 1992 eliminating Bloodsworth as the perpetrator of the crime. He served over eight years in prison until his release in 1993. He was the first person to be exonerated from death row through post-conviction DNA analysis. Kirk works today with the Innocence Project to lobby for criminal justice reform involving wrongful persecution.

Kirk Bloodworth was the first person to be exonerated from death row using post-conviction DNA testing.

Summary

The Innocence Project was founded in 1992 by attorneys Paul Neufeld and Barry Scheck. The mission of the project is to exonerate inmates wrongly convicted of crimes through DNA analysis. Kirk Bloodsworth was convicted and serving a death row sentence when he was eliminated as the perpetrator of the brutal rape and murder of a nine year old girl in 1984. He was the first person to be exonerated from death row using post-conviction DNA analysis after serving eight years in prison.

· ·

Concept Reinforcement

1. What is the mission of the Innocence Project?

2. What prompted the founding of the Innocence Project?

3. How are candidates selected for participation in the Innocence Project?

Appendix

Concept Reinforcement Answer Key

Chapter 1

1. The application of science as it relates to the law.

2. Physical science and medical sciences

3. Forensics developed as scientists and law enforcement personnel learned how to collect and analyze evidence.

Chapter 2

1. Crime labs are held to even higher standards than research and clinical labs because the work of the crime lab affects criminal proceedings and must withstand the scrutiny of a defense attorney. The crime lab must ensure complete compliance with all ethical standards, and all evidence handling and analysis protocols. Any break in these ethical standards or evidence handling protocols can damage the criminal case, potentially resulting in the case being dismissed because the evidence was compromised.

2. A full service crime lab will usually include 5 basic service units: physical science unit, biology unit, firearms unit (ballistics), document examination unit, and photography unit. A full service lab may also include a toxicology unit, a latent fingerprint unit, a polygraph unit, a voiceprint analysis unit, and an evidence collection unit.

3. The Physical Sciences Unit analyzes the physical evidence from the crime scene. This does not include biological samples. The Physical Science Unit performs tests on samples, such as drugs, glass, paint, soil, and explosives.

Chapter 3

1. Forensic Investigator: responsible for collecting bodies from crime scenes, preparing bodies for transport, attempting to identify the body, collecting personal belongings, interviewing friends, family members and other witnesses, collecting evidence from the body before transport, preparing written reports on actions taken, and possibly testifying in court.

    Forensic Pathology Technician: A pathology technician assists the forensic pathologist in performing autopsies. They may even perform parts of the autopsy. A forensic pathology technician collects samples for toxicology testing, as well as tissues for microscopic examination (histology), blood for blood testing, samples to test for infectious diseases, fingerprints, X-rays, and trace evidence analysis. In some cases, forensic pathology technicians interact with the families of victims and the police.

Fingerprint Examiner: A person in this position is responsible for collecting and analyzing fingerprints. This is a key position in any crime lab. In order to do this job, you must understand how to find, collect and protect fingerprint evidence, as well as how to analyze it and match it to an individual.

Forensic Medical Transcriber: A forensic medical transcriber is responsible for transcribing oral and written notes on autopsies or other forensic tests. The job also includes other administrative duties like filing, interacting with the public, and record keeping. This is an important position for maintaining the efficiency of the coroner's office and professionalism of the coroner's office.

Forensic Document Examiner: A forensic document examiner is responsible for examining document for age, authenticity and authorship. A person in this position must be able to work alone and also be extremely patient and detail-oriented. Skills required include photography, language and lab testing procedures.

Criminalist: Criminalist is a modern term that usually refers to crime scene and crime lab workers. People who are attracted to this field usually enjoy law enforcement and the precision of laboratory work.

2. A forensic pathologist must have a medical degree, which is followed by a medical internship (1 year) and a pathology residency (4 years). After all this education, you still need to pass the forensic pathology board exams to be certified in anatomic pathology and forensic pathology if you want to lead the lab. This exam is administered by the American Board of Pathology.

3. All of the positions in a crime lab contribute in unique ways to solving crimes.

Chapter 4

1. First responders determine whether a crime has taken place. If they determine that a crime has taken place, they secure the scene and call the crime scene investigators. The police, who are typically the first responders, work with the crime scene investigators to secure the crime scene; identify, protect and collect the evidence; ensure the chain of custody of the evidence; and transport it to the crime lab. If a death occurred, the forensic investigator or medical examiner is called to prepare the body for transport, collect evidence from the body, try to identify the body, and interview witnesses.

2. Local law enforcement agencies may not have the resources they need to fully process a crime scene. In these cases, they will collaborate with nearby jurisdictions, state labs, or other law enforcement and forensic agencies.

3. The state police and state crime labs serve law enforcement needs throughout a state. State Patrols are usually responsible for highway safety and providing statewide law enforcement services, including assistance to local law enforcement if they need help. State crime labs provide forensic analysis services to law enforcement agencies statewide.

Chapter 5

1. The FBI Laboratory supports the US Criminal Justice System at all levels.

2. The mission of CIL is to search for, recover, and identify US personnel missing from past military conflicts.

3. The databases provide comprehensive information on DNA (CODIS – FBI), the frequency of eyeglass prescriptions in the population (OptoSearch – CIL), and dental records (OdontoSearch - CIL). These databases are available for forensic laboratories to help identify individuals from remains or evidence collected by the labs.

Chapter 6

1. The mission of INTERPOL is to facilitate cross border police cooperation, and to support and assist all organizations, authorities and services with a mission to prevent or combat crime.

2. INTERPOL was established after World War I, when Europe experienced a massive crime wave due to the weak economy after the war ended. INTERPOL is the modern form of the law enforcement organization formed at the 1923 when Johann Schober, head of the Vienna police department, called for international cooperation between police departments.

3. Many crimes cross national borders, therefore becoming international crimes. This means that the law enforcement agencies of the nations involved must cooperate if they want to apprehend and prosecute the criminals.

Chapter 7

1. The first person to arrive at the crime scene determines whether a crime has occurred. If a crime has occurred, the crime scene is identified and secured, evidence is collected, logged and transported following specific protocols to protect the evidence and ensure the chain of custody. Witnesses are identified and interviewed.

2. Photography documents the scene, witnesses and victims of the crime. They capture the crime scene before it is altered by the investigators and are careful to use points of reference to maintain proper perspective. Photography can be still or video.

   Sketches document the locations of different items related to the crime, showing the relationships between the objects, the position and location of any bodies, and the distances between objects. They typically have legends that describe the key objects in the scene. Measurements must be accurate even if the sketch is rough.

   Notes are taken by a designated note taker, who is responsible for documenting the crime scene, including all activities at the scene. This can be done using note pads or tape recorders.

3. Frame of reference is essential in reconstructing the crime and performing evidence analysis. The analyst will test the theories she develops against the evidence to make sure it makes sense. Frame of reference is essential to this testing process.

Chapter 8

1. Contact between two items will always result in an exchange between the items.

2. Trace evidence is any material related to a crime scene. It may be nearly invisible, but can be essential to solving a crime. Therefore, it is essential to minimize crime scene contamination so that any evidence collected is actually related to the crime and not the result of contamination after the crime occurred

3. Bone fragments, teeth, hair, skin, fingerprints, fibers, glass, paint chips, soils, metals, botanical materials, gunshot residue

Chapter 9

1. Fragile evidence is most likely to be lost, damaged or contaminated.

2. Each piece of evidence is packaged separately to prevent cross-contamination and damage to the samples.

3. The chain of custody is a continuous record of the evidence. The record shows that the evidence was controlled (kept safe and secure) during transport from the crime scene to the lab and then to the courtroom. If the chain of custody is broken, the evidence may not be admissible in court.

Chapter 10

1. Physical evidence is any evidence that is non-living or inorganic.

2. Chemistry is used to determine the specific composition of drugs, explosives, and other evidence, which might provide investigators clues about the source of the evidence.

3. Rope is made from different materials and is made in different ways (braiding, twisting). Tape has different compositions, widths, adhesives and tear pattern characteristics. All of these pieces of information can be used to compare to evidence when trying to solve a crime.

Chapter 11

1. Crime scene reconstruction is used to figure out the events that led up to the crime or occurred during the crime.

2. Specific Incident Reconstruction, Specific Event Reconstruction, Specific Physical Evidence Reconstruction

3. If the evidence of the crime does not fit the theory of the crime, the theory is adjusted until it matches the evidence. The result of the analysis is the reconstruction of the crime, including the assessment of how likely the crime can be shown to have occurred according to the theory of the crime.

Chapter 12

1. Physical evidence analysis is important to solving crimes because it can match weapons to injuries; fingerprints to individuals; tire tracks to tires and vehicles, stab wounds to weapons, bite marks to individuals, etc. Blood spatter can be used to understand the location of the victim and the criminal.

2. It is important to remain objective because evidence may appear to show one scenario, especially at a staged crime scene, but be proved to show another scenario based on accurate, careful and objective analysis.

3. These checklists are useful to investigators because they help ensure that all the necessary steps, documentation and procedures are followed when handling and analyzing evidence. This is essential to supporting the prosecution case in criminal trials.

Chapter 13

1. The 6th Amendment to the US Constitution guarantees the accused the right to a speedy and public trial.

2. The Magna Carta described common law, which is the concept that all citizens, regardless of social status, must follow certain legal procedures, respect certain rights and accept that all people are subject to the rule of law. This led to the 6th Amendment of the US Constitution.

3. A criminal trial is designed to ensure that the accused receives a fair trial based on the available evidence. Decisions may be made by judge or jury. In most cases, a jury trial is chosen. Evidence is included or excluded based on legal standards. Each side makes opening statements, which are followed by presentation of the prosecution case, which includes calling witnesses, cross examination and redirect. The prosecution, when finished presenting, will rest and will often move to dismiss the case. Most of these motions are denied. The defense then presents its case in the same manner as the prosecution case. Once the defense rests, the prosecution is allowed to rebut the defense case. The attorneys and the judge settle on jury instructions, after which closing arguments are presented by each side. The prosecution has a chance to rebut the defense's closing argument. Once the closing arguments are complete, the judge delivers jury instructions, the jury deliberates and finds the defendant guilty or not guilty. At this point, post-trial motions, if any are made and the judge rules on them, and any sentencing activities are carried out.

Chapter 14

1. An expert witness is someone who has more knowledge about a topic than an average person. This expertise allows him to give testimony on an issue that is important to the case. Expert witnesses must have the credentials and experience to prove their expert status.

2. Frye v. United States resulted in the Frye Standard.
   Daubert v. Merrell-Dow Pharmaceuticals, Inc., resulted in Rule 702 of the Federal Rules of Evidence.

3. Forensic experts provide expert testimony and education. They can help explain the complex scientific information resulting from the forensic analysis in terms that a lay audience is able to understand.

Chapter 15

1. The police often need to prevent information about specific aspects of a crime from being released to the public because an unusual aspect of a crime can help identify the perpetrator or provide a link to other crimes. It is important to prevent undue influence from the media on crime scene investigators or forensic analysts. The media may pressure people involved in the case to release information before it is presented at trial or before the police have identified the perpetrator. Premature release of information related to a crime can compromise the investigation and the ability of the police to find, arrest and prosecute the offender.

2. There is a general agreement that live television coverage:
   1. Distracts trial participants.
   2. Unfairly affects the outcome of a trial.
   3. Diminishes the integrity of the courts.

3. The purpose of the sunshine, or Freedom of Information Act, laws is to allow reporters to request information about police investigations under FOIA. This means that the agency receiving the request has the burden of proof if they want to withhold any information.

Chapter 16

1. CSI's collect and preserve evidence and then transport it to the crime lab for testing.

2. Camera, tape, ruler, sketch pad, pens, protective gear, flashlight, UV light, evidence bags, fingerprinting kit, casting kit, etc.

3. It's important so that it can be used as evidence in a trial.

Chapter 17

1. Forensic pathologists will perform autopsies, attend death scenes, and study many disciplines of forensics including ballistics, serology, toxicology, odontology, radiology, and anthropology. The most important function performed by a forensic pathologist is deciding how and why a person died.

2. Proximate cause of death is the underlying or original condition that led to the immediate cause of death.

3. Homicide, suicide, accident, natural, undetermined

Chapter 18

1. To determine the cause and manner of death.

2. Rigor mortis is the stiffening of the muscles following death. Immediately after death occurs, the muscles are flaccid (loose). Livor mortis (also known as lividity) is the discoloration of portions of the body after death due to the settling of blood in the tissues. These variables can help a pathologist determine an estimated time of death.

3. To examine the organs and tissues in order to determine the cause of death.

Chapter 19

1. Fingerprints consist of the unique friction ridges found on the palm surface of the fingers and thumbs.

2. Visible, latent, and plastic prints

3. A fingerprint analyst conducts a point-by-point comparison of ridge characteristics between two prints. An average of 12 ridge characteristic matches needs to be charted in order to make a positive match between two prints.

Chapter 20

1. Is it blood?
   Is it human in origin?
   Who does the blood belong to?

2. Gunshot wound

3. By utilizing the angle of convergence

Chapter 21

1. Shoe impressions, tire tread impressions, and tool marks

2. A cast or a mold is made of the print.

3. A comparison microscope is used to match the marking made.

Chapter 22

1. Trace evidence is left due to the contact of objects or substances with one another through contact friction. The most commonly collected trace evidence includes hairs, glass, paint chips/flecks, fibers, dirt/dust/soil, plant materials, and explosive chemicals.

2. From looking at the root of a hair, a criminalist can tell if it fell out naturally or was pulled out. Hair examination can reveal if the hair is in fact human or from another animal species. The hair root may contain DNA that can be used for comparison purposes later on.

3. Comparison microscope

Chapter 23

1. They are responsible for making comparisons of bullets and casings found at a scene, and also participate in the following important tasks:
   • Restoration of obscured serial numbers
   • Detection of gunpowder residues on garments and surrounding wounds
   • Estimation of distance between gun and target during firing of a weapon
   • Detection of gunpowder residues on hands of suspected shooters

2. Comparison microscope

3. They can tell the distance between the shooter and victim and it can indicate if someone has fired a gun or handled a weapon that was recently fired.

Chapter 24

1. ABO and rH

2. A-antigen and Anti-B antibody

3. It can be used as a means to eliminate suspects and include other suspects for further DNA testing.

Chapter 25

1. A molecule of DNA appears microscopically like a twisted ladder otherwise known as a double helix. Each side of the ladder is made up of alternating phosphates and sugars (deoxyribose sugar). The rungs of the ladder are composed of pairs of nucleotide bases called adenine (A), guanine (G), thymine (T), and cytosine (C).

2. To avoid contamination of the sample

3. The Combined DNA Index System (CODIS) is a database that stores 13 specified STR points of convicted criminals that can be used for comparison with a sample from a crime scene.

Chapter 26

1. The detection and identification of drugs and/or poisons in the body fluids, tissues, and organs. This can include testing urine, blood, saliva, hair, fingernails, or other tissue samples from the body.

2. Blood alcohol level

3. Carbon Monoxide (CO)

Chapter 27

1. Arson is considered the purposeful act of starting a fire or explosion in order to do harm to a person, multiple persons, or property.

2. FBI Bomb database and the ATF Arson and Explosives National Repository

3. Indiscriminate killers, non-specific targets, desire to watch the aftermath of their work

Chapter 28

1. An organic substance contains carbon in combination with other elements such as hydrogen, oxygen, nitrogen, phosphorus, or chlorine.

2. Chromatography is a common technique used to purify substances that contain multiple components.

3. The mass spectrophotometer (mass spec) is a very complex piece of equipment used in forensic science for chemical analysis. Once a mixture is separated by chromatography, the mass spec can identify extremely small quantities of substances present within the mixture.

Chapter 29

1. An object that contains handwriting or printing whose authenticity or original source is in question.

2. angularity, slope, speed, pressure, letter formation, word spacing, letter dimensions, connections, pen movements, writing skills, and finger dexterity

3. Using infrared photography techniques

Chapter 30

1. Through the use of a recording device

2. The voice print of an individual that measures the pitch, volume, and resonance of a human voice.

3. When Howard Hughes called in to declare it as a fake, the authorities used voice analysis to verify that it was indeed Howard Hughes.

Chapter 31

1. Forensic odontology is forensic dentistry. It is a branch of forensic medicine that properly examines, handles, and presents dental evidence in a court of law.

2. Forensic odontologists use a range of tools to identify individual skeletal remains. These include dental x-rays, casts, photographs, imaging tools, computer graphics tools, and databases. These tools allow forensic odontologists to match skeletal remains with the records of known individuals because each person's dentition is unique.

3. Bite marks can be used to match bit wounds to an individual, as well as bite patterns found in food evidence.

Chapter 32

1. Forensic anthropology is a field of forensic science that applies physical anthropology principles and techniques to the legal process.

2. Forensic anthropologists are able to determine age, sex, ancestry, stature, health history and lifestyle of the individual, the age of the skeletal remains, the whether an injury was the cause of death, the time of death and even the number of individuals in a mass grave. Specialists in this field study more than the remains. They also study the environment in which the remains are found. The environment can provide significant clues to the circumstances of death. These include items found in or near the grave site, such as buttons, jewelry, clothing, and anything else that might help identify the individual.

3. A biological profile is a reconstruction of the person's life and death, including biological sex, chronological age, ante-mortem trauma, ancestry and stature. Forensic anthropologists use their training and extensive databases of bone characteristics to build the biological profile. The biological profile helps narrow the potential matches to the individual represented by the remains.

Chapter 33

1. Forensic entomology uses the knowledge of insect life cycles and habitats to determine the approximate time of death and whether the body was moved from one location to another. Forensic entomologists specialize in flies and other insects that feed on corpses.

2. Insects tend to show up at a corpse in a predictable pattern. This pattern varies from place to place, but is consistent for a specific location. Geographic region, locale, time of day and season all affect the behavioral and developmental patterns of insects. In addition, some insects are there to feed on the corpse, while others are there to eat the first insects that showed up. Forensic entomologists are able to determine time since death based on all the variables that affect the insect behavior for that particular area. They can also determine whether a body was moved based on the types of insects found on the corpse.

3. Scanning electron microscopy is used to identify specific species of fly eggs found on a corpse, especially when the corpse is very fresh. Gene expression is used to assess the developmental stage of the insects based on which genes are active and which are not active. This information can be used to determine the post-mortem interval.

Chapter 34

1. Forensic psychiatry is a branch of psychiatry that is adversarial rather than therapeutic. Forensic psychiatry works to dissect the personality and motives of the accused.

2. A forensic psychiatric evaluation will generally include the following:
Complete medical history
Psychiatric medical status examination Psychological assessment
Review of pertinent medical records, discovery and evidentiary deposition transcripts, school records, work product, and any related materials.
The results of neuropsychological tests

A forensic brain injury evaluation is done in cases where brain injury is obvious or suspected. The brain injury may be a result of trauma, loss of oxygen (hypoxia), stroke (ischemia), or toxins/chemicals. The evaluations will generally include the following:
Neurological Exam
Neuropsychological assessment
Structural and/or functional brain images
Lab studies

3. Brain imaging signals are interpreted using a model, which is based on a set of assumptions. This allows clinicians to draw inferences, but not make a definitive statement, about a patient. The procedures used for brain imaging are not standardized and can be easily manipulated by someone with the appropriate technical expertise. Additionally, the definition of "normal" is elusive. It may mean the exclusion of physiological or psychological disease and it is not clear where abnormal actually becomes dysfunctional.

Chapter 35

1. Forensic profiling is the process of looking at evidence and making a best guess about the type of individual who would commit the crime.

2. A forensic profiler uses all the evidence found at a crime scene (physical, behavioral, psychiatric) to develop a picture of the offender, including the modus operandi and any signature.

   The profiler goes through a process of asking questions and obtaining answers, such as the following:
   How did the criminal gain access to the crime scene or the victim?
   What did the criminal do?
   Did the criminal try to hide his tracks?
   Why was the victim or crime scene attractive to the criminal?
   What was the criminal's motive?

3. Crime scene analysis
       1. Profiling inputs
       2. Decision process models
       3. Crime assessment
       4. Criminal Profile
       5. Investigation
       6. Apprehensions

   Behavioral evidence analysis
       1. Equivocal forensic analysis
       2. Victimology
       3. Crime scene characteristics
       4. Offender characteristics

Chapter 36

1. Forensic interviewing is used when questioning the alleged victims of child abuse or adult sexual abuse. Forensic interviewing is different than interrogation, which is used by the police when questioning suspected criminals. The primary purpose of a forensic interview is to find out if the victim was, in fact, mistreated. The key secondary purpose of the forensic interview is to collect evidence that will stand up in court.

2. The forensic interviewer must remain objective in order to collect evidence that will be acceptable during a trial.

3. Forced choice questions limit the respondent to a certain number of answer choices, such as yes or no. An invitational question, which is also called an open-ended question, allow the subject to answer in whatever way the subject chooses. These questions allow the subject to say as much or as little as he or she chooses.

Chapter 37

1. Forensic engineering is the application of the art and science of engineering to matters of law.

2. Forensic engineers follow the scientific method to ensure that they perform a thorough, objective investigation that will stand up in court.

3. Forensic engineers investigate vehicle speeds, component failure, construction equipment failures, crashworthiness, mechanical design, mechanical equipment failures, occupant kinematics (movement), occupant restraint analysis, vehicle dynamics, and visibility analysis.

Chapter 38

1. Digital forensics is the application of digital and computer technologies to matters of law.

2. 1. Usually latent (unseen).
   2. Can move across borders easily
   3. Is fragile and can be altered or destroyed easily.
   4. Is sometimes time sensitive.

3. Criminal investigations:
   1. Child pornography
   2. Homicides
   3. Embezzlement
   4. Financial Fraud
   Civil cases:
   1. Fraud
   2. Divorce
   3. Breach of contract
   4. Copyright

Chapter 39

1. Forensic accounting combines accounting, auditing and investigative skills in the context of the legal system.

2. Investigative Accounting is used to investigate criminal matters. The primary goal is to determine whether a financial crime has occurred.

3. 1. Investigating and analyzing financial evidence
   2. Developing computerized applications to help with analyzing and presenting financial evidence.
   3. Present their findings using reports, exhibits, and document collections.
   4. Assisting with legal proceedings, including providing testimony in court and preparing visual aids for use in the trial.

Chapter 40

1. Dogs, which are the primary animals used as animal investigators, have much better hearing than humans and are better able to differentiate between scents and detect a specific scent even in the presence of dozens of other scents.

2. 1. Take you in a direction that is away from the crime scene.
   2. Give you a path to follow to search for other items related to the crime.
   3. Lead you to footprints or tire prints, which can then be collected.
   4. Lead you to a subject and identify the individual.

3. Tracking: Locating and following a scent to find a person and/or crime scene.
   Article Search: Using the scent of an article or group of articles in an attempt to locate the crime scene.

Chapter 41

1. 911 call from Nicole Brown Simpson showing the violent tendency of OJ Simpson in the past.
   Hairs consistent with Simpson are fond in the cap at the Bundy crime scene
   Hairs consistent with Simpson are found on the shirt of Ron Goldman
   Fibers consistent with the carpet in Simpson's bronco from the Bundy crime scene
   Blood matching Simpson's found near the footprints found at the Bundy crime scene.
   Fresh cuts on Simpson's fingers the day after the crime.
   Blood found in OJ's Bronco, in foyer, master bedroom, driveway and on OJ's socks at his home matching the murder victims.
   Left glove found at crime scene and matching right glove found at Simpson's house. Shoe prints found at Bunch crime scene matched a pair of size 12 shoes that Simpson was known to have.
   Flight away from arrest in Bronco.
   Strange reaction to phone call informing him of Nicole's death.

2. Faulty evidence collection procedures. A police trainee that helped to gather the blood samples had carried them in his lab coat pocket for the entire day before turning it in as an exhibit.

3. Four (4) hours.

Chapter 42

1. White collar crime has been defined as a type of crime that is committed by a person of considerable respectability or high social status in the course of their occupation. This includes corporate crimes such as those involving fraud, embezzlement, bribery, insider trading, forgery, and computer crimes. These crimes involve deceit and not physical violence.

2. Bank Fraud: An act or consistent pattern with the purpose of defrauding a bank of funds.
    Blackmail: The demand for money or other priority treatment through the use of physical threat or exposure of confidential information.
    Bribery: The use of money, goods, or services offered in exchange for personal influence or action of another person or entity. A person can be tried for taking a bribe or offering one.
    Cellular Phone Fraud: The illegal tampering or unauthorized use of a cellular phone. This includes stealing the valid ESN number from one cellular phone and transferring it to another.
    Computer Fraud: A crime committed by a computer hacker to steal information such as bank account numbers, credit card numbers, or other confidential information.
    Counterfeiting: When an individual copies a specific article and attempts to pass it as genuine. This includes money, watches, designer's bags, artwork, or other valuable assets.
    Credit Card Fraud: The illegal use of another person's credit card to purchase goods or services.
    Embezzlement: When an individual who has been entrusted with a certain amount of money or valuables uses it for their own benefit.
    Extortion: When an individual obtains property illegally by threatening force or violence.
    Forgery: When an individual passes a fake element such as a check with the intent to defraud the recipient.
    Health Care Fraud: When an unlicensed individual provides health care services to others and gains monetarily for the services.
    Insider Trading When an individual uses confidential, non-disclosed information to trade in shares from a public company.
    Insurance Fraud: An individual gains monetary benefits by deceiving an insurance company, for instance faking an injury on the job.
    Investment Schemes: When an individual promises to gain large returns on a small investment as a ploy to steal money.
    Kickback: When an individual sells an item and pays back a portion of the price to the buyer.
    Investment Schemes: When an individual promises to gain large returns on a small investment as a ploy to steal money.
    Larceny/Theft: The wrongful taking of another person's property.
    Investment Schemes: When an individual promises to gain large returns on a small investment as a ploy to steal money.
    Money Laundering: The investment or transfer of money gained through illegal activity that is made to appear legitimate.
    Racketeering: The engagement in illegal activities (i.e. selling drugs) for personal financial gain.
    Securities Fraud: The artificial inflation of a stock price by brokers so individuals will believe they are buying stocks on the rise.

Tax Evasion: When an individual purposely evades paying taxes or falsifies their returns. Telemarketing Fraud: Individuals place telephone calls to businesses or residences in an attempt to gain monetarily by alleging they are collecting for a charity or other organization. Welfare Fraud: The act of taking welfare benefits under illegal circumstances.

3. A Ponzi scheme is a type of investment scam where an individual solicits the investment of others into a proposed business venture or stock. A high return rate is promised in exchange for the investment. However, the perpetrator never invests the money and instead appears to pay dividends by using newly recruited investors money. The scheme ends once the scam has run out of new investors to pay old investor dividends or the perpetrator flees town with the money.

Chapter 43

1. The attacks did not follow any specific pattern.

2. Every piece was handmade using items that could be found in any local hardware store. The bomber included the letters "FC" stamped into some aspect of the metal pieces of the bomb.

3. The Unabomber's brother, Ted Kaczynski, turned him in to the FBI.

Chapter 44

1. A cold case is a crime or accident that has not yet been solved and is not currently the subject of a criminal investigation.

2. A cold case may be re-opened after new evidence surfaces or when new technology is available that makes it possible to do new tests on the evidence.

3. Submission of a work order written by Oba Chandler that matched the handwritten directions that were part of the evidence of the crime. The handwriting matched.

Chapter 45

1. The Innocence Project is a national organization that is dedicated to exonerating individuals who have been wrongly convicted of a crime by using DNA evidence.

2. Development of DNA testing technology that was reliable enough to test samples from old cases.

3. They are subjected to a lengthy screening process to determine if DNA evidence could be useful in proving their claims of innocence.

Made in the USA
Columbia, SC
01 September 2021